Social Security: Maximize Your Benefits

Kathleen Sindell, Ph.D.

Kathleen Sindell, Ph.D.

ISBN-10: 1475089457
ISBN-13: 978-1475089455

DEDICATION

To my family: Ivan my loving husband; Devon, Tate, Annabelle and Aubrey who are always interested in my projects; Michal, Rich, Rico and Ruby who are distant but close to my heart.

CONTENTS AT A GLANCE

EXTENDED TABLE OF CONTENTS

Kathleen Sindell, Ph.D.

ACKNOWLEDGEMENTS

I am indebted to the following people who brought their expertise to bear on this book. Deborah Kraut improved the text with her careful editing and keen insights. Deborah is a current annuitant who retired in 2011. The precise technical editing of elder law services attorney Leda Gottlieb, advocate for seniors and the disabled, greatly improved the work. Leda Gottlieb can be contacted at www.zetlinlaw.com or at 703-379-0442.

I am grateful to my associates, students, friends and family who have discussed how Social Security has affected their lives and given me a better understanding of what folks need to know before claiming Social Security retirement benefits.

Thank you all for your wonderful help in bringing this book to publication. Of course, I am responsible for any errors.

Feedback, Please

I expect that over time and with new legislation there will be new claiming strategies, changes to current strategies and an end to some of the existing claiming approaches. I am seeking your feedback about what worked for you in your personal financial situation. For example, when implementing your claiming strategy, did you reformulate it in a unique way? Are you a financial adviser who would like to reveal an exceptional claiming approach? If you would like to share your personal story or if you have questions please contact me at ksindell@kathleensindell.com.

Disclaimers

Examples used throughout "<u>Social Security: Maximize Your Benefits</u>" are fictional. Any resemblance to actual persons, living or dead is purely coincidental.

The opinions expressed in "<u>Social Security: Maximize Your Benefits</u>" are the author's own. They do not represent the positions of the publisher, Social Security Administration, any professional association, or educational institution.

INTRODUCTION

Who this Book is for

This book is written for you, you and the thousands of folks like you who will soon be living on fixed incomes. Many of you are unaware of the Social Security retirement benefits to which you are entitled. The Social Security Handbook has 2,728 rules governing benefits. The Program Operating System (POMs) has thousands more. It is no wonder that you do not have a good understanding of Social Security. Frequently, because of a lack of insight you do not receive all the benefits you could receive. Often the problem is that you can only check on things you know about. Social Security representatives can answer questions but cannot provide advice about your personal financial situation.

Knowing the right questions to ask is critical to maximizing your Social Security benefits. To sum it up, this book is written for the people who need more information about the claiming strategies that provide the most benefits for their circumstances.

According to the Social Security Administration (SSA) in 2009, 72 percent of the 2.7 million new filers claimed Social Security retirement benefits early. In 2007 and 2008, 74 percent also filed early (this is the highest number ever recorded). In 1980, just 57 percent filed early and in 1970, 47 percent claimed benefits early.

For some filing for early retirement was the right choice. But, for most claimants, early retirement results in the loss of billions of dollars, in that they have not sought professional advice or researched optimal strategies to maximize their benefits. This book sets the reader on a path to learning about how to develop an optimal claiming strategy. The advantages and limitations of different claiming approaches are examined so that the reader can clearly see the risks and rewards of claiming at different times, working after full retirement age (FRA), and how longevity plays a major role in selecting the optimal approach.

Why this Book at this Time?

According to the well-known *2012 Retirement Confidence Survey Factsheet* (May 2012) developed by the Employee Benefit Research Institute located in Washington, DC many workers reported that they had little or no savings and investments.

Table I.1 shows in the last five years Americans have been saving and investing more but the amount is not nearly enough to fund an estimated 30 to 35 years of retirement. Additionally, about 60 percent of the workers surveyed for the *Factsheet* reported that the total value of their household savings and investments (excluding their primary home) and any defined benefit plan was less than $25,000.

Table I.1 Few Americans are Prepared for Retirement

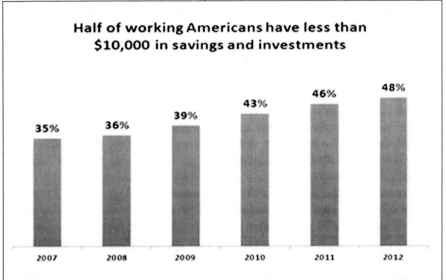

SOURRCE: *2012 Retirement Confidence Survey Factsheet*, Employee Benefits Research Institute (tcf.org/retirement/social-security), 2012.

The *Factsheet* continues by stating that approximately half of the current retirees surveyed had left the work force unexpectedly due to health issues, disability, or employment changes, such as downsizing or closure. The *Factsheet* declares that retirees are significantly more reliant on Social Security benefits as a source of income. (To read the *2012 Retirement Confidence Survey Factsheet* see www.ebri.org/publications/ib/index.cfm?content_id=5017&fa=ibDisp.)

To my way of thinking, the *2012 Retirement Confidence Survey Factsheet* highlights why it is more important than ever to make certain that the claiming strategy you select is the optimal approach for your individual financial situation. Maximizing your Social Security benefits can result in thousands of dollars added to your income over your retirement years.

If you Need Help Implementing Your Optimal Claiming Strategy

According to *Kiplinger's Personal Finance* magazine (Sheedy and Garland, April 2011) not all Social Security personnel are familiar with optimal claiming strategies. Sheedy and Garland cite the experience of a couple who used the Restricted Application methodology (detailed in this book in Chapter 5: Maximizing your Benefits by Claiming Now and Claiming More Later) when claiming benefits.

The Social Security Web site provides the specifics of this methodology at www.socialsecurity.gov/retire2/yourspouse.htm. (Look at the section called, "If you or your spouse is full retirement age.") When the couple presented their claiming strategy to a Social Security representative they were told that the FRA wife could not restrict her application to spousal benefits only. After being turned down several times, the couple reached out to Kiplinger's staff and with help from another Social Security Representative their application strategy was finally approved.

It is difficult, if not impossible, for any one person (including this author) to be an expert on each rule. If your local Social Security office cannot provide you with the assistance you need, the next step is to contact your Congressman. For example, Representative Buck McKeon of the 25th District of California has a special Web page that invites his constituents to contact him about Social Security issues. The Representative McKeon's Social Security Web page provides guidelines and a downloadable Privacy Release Form so his staff can quickly get to work on your behalf (for more information see mckeonforms.house.gov/Casework/SocialSecurity.htm).

Contacting your Representative for Help with Social Security

You may encounter issues with Social Security that require the help of your Congressman. Go online to www.house.gov/representatives/ for the House of Representatives Directory. At the top right corner, enter your zip code. A Web page with the name and description of your representative will appear. Click on the name of your representative to go to the representative's Web page. In the Search Box on the representative's page enter "Social Security". The search results will point you in the right direction. Once you are on the page that you desire, you'll find the contact information for the representative's office. Ask for the staffer who is in charge of Social Security issues.

How this Book is Organized

This book focuses on strategies to maximize Social Security retirement benefits.

It does not cover other government programs such as Medicare and disability, as well as, civil service pensions, and military service pensions.

Each chapter stands alone or you can read the book from beginning to end. The goal of each chapter is to focus on what you can do to maximize your monthly benefits. You will discover many activities that you can do today to increase your benefits. For example, you can use the SSA's online estimator to assess the amount of future benefits you can expect using different claiming strategies, become skilled at downloading your personal Social Security statement 24 hours a day seven days a week to review your earnings history to make any needed corrections, and take advantage of the SSAs online calculator to estimate your longevity (so that you don't outlive your resources).

Summaries of Chapter 1 Through Chapter 9

This introduction is designed to provide you with summaries of the chapters so that you can zero in on the issue(s) that interest you the most. Once you have found the answer you are seeking you can expand your reading to the chapters that cover similar subjects or you can read the book from beginning to end.

Chapter 1: Increasing Your Benefits by Selecting the "Right" Application Date

This chapter reviews the increased importance of Social Security retirement benefits. Readers look into who is eligible for Social Security benefits, the Social Security credit system, how to download your individual Social Security Statement and make any necessary corrections. Next you'll see how longevity affects the optimal age for claiming benefits. The chapter goes on to examine how early retirement reduces benefits for the claimant and his or her spouse. The reduction of benefits for early retirees is further explored in a comparison table of cumulative payments to age 95 for an individual who retires at 62, FRA and 70. Next you'll see how to calculate the break-even age for early retirement. In other words, at what age will the early retiree receive less benefits than if he or she retired at FRA. The chapter goes on to show how early retirees have to pay taxes on their benefits and illustrates what the SSA includes as taxable "earned income". The chapter concludes by stating that currently individuals can earn a benefit increase of 8 percent per year by delaying claiming benefits. Additionally, the increased monthly benefit raises the first survivor benefit. Therefore delaying claiming benefits until 70 is the easiest way to increase monthly benefits.

Chapter 2: Increasing Your Benefits by Utilizing Spousal and Family Benefits

Using spousal benefits is often an easy way to hike monthly Social Security benefits. This chapter shows how the SSA defines spouse, ex-spouse, dependent children and parents. You'll grasp how to calculate the family maximum benefit (which is about 150 to 180 percent of the worker's benefit amount). You'll grasp how the earner's and ex-spouse's benefits are not included in the family maximum benefit. You'll discover how to calculate the family maximum benefit, see examples of early spousal benefits, and establish the impact of a worker's early retirement on the early retirement of his or her spouse. Next you'll become aware of "Dual Entitlement". Dual entitlement allows a spouse, ex-spouse or survivor to claim benefits on their own work record or on the earner's work record. The chapter concludes with instructions about how to maximize benefits by determining if you should claim your own benefits or your spousal benefit.

Chapter 3: Maximizing Survivor Benefits

This chapter helps individuals identify the definitions and eligibility rules of survivors in traditional and non-traditional unions. You'll see how the definitions and eligibility requirements for survivors are similar to spouses, ex-spouses and dependent children (and how there are a few striking differences). Combined family maximum limits are explored and the taxation of survivor benefits is discussed. Next the differences between fully insured and currently insured survivor benefits are reviewed. Survivor eligibility requirements and benefit amounts are considered for several survivors early retirement scenarios. Numerous survivor claiming strategies are explored and compared. Optimal claiming strategies based for a deceased non-FRA worker and a young widow(er) and FRA widow(er) are examined. In addition to optimal claiming strategies for a deceased FRA worker and a young widow(er) and FRA widow(er).

Chapter 4: Getting More by Retracting Your Application and Refiling (The "Reset")

Before December 8, 2010 the "Reset" was a popular way to give yourself an "interest-free" loan. However, new regulations limit this option and increase the risk of this approach. This is how it works, during the first 12-months that you begin to receive Social Security benefits you can withdraw your application. This is a once in a lifetime SSA approved option. Let's say that you apply for benefits on your 62nd birthday. You are nearing your 63rd birthday and you realize that you have to go back to work. To stop benefits use the one-page request form titled, "Withdrawal Application Form SSA-521". The benefit of this strategy is that it is similar to buying an immediate annuity, except that you don't have to pay any interest on the benefits you have already received. The difficulty of this strategy is that you'll need the cash on-hand to pay back the benefits you received. However, for some folks that have assets, need cash and would have to pay a high penalty for "cashing out" early this approach may be a viable option.

Chapter 5: "Claim Now and Claim More Later" to Boost Monthly Benefits

The "Restricted Application" approach is often called the "Claim Now and Claim More Later" strategy. This is a "married only" approach that works when one of the spouses is FRA. This method is best when the low earner claims benefits, the FRA high earner files for his or her own benefits and immediately "restricts" the application and claims spousal benefits on the low earner's work record. The high earner collects spousal benefits and accrues Delayed Retirement Credits (DRCs) from 66 to 70. At age 70 the high earner re-applies and claims benefits on his or her own work record. Many experts state that at this time the low earner spouse can claim spousal benefits on the high earner's work record. However, before taking any action check with a financial professional to verify that the low earner spouse can change accounts. The benefits of the restricted application approach, if the high earner works for four years after FRA, include an increase to the FRA benefit of 32 percent. The DRCs will also increase the first death survivor benefit and provide a higher base for annual Cost-Of-Living-increases (COLAs). This approach is especially effective for ex-spouses who "want to catch-up" and plan to work until 70. Ex-spouses can use the restricted application strategy to increase their retirement nest eggs even if the ex-spouse does not file for benefits. Claiming strategies can get pretty complicated. The Internet provides several sources of optimal claiming strategy calculators and software programs. Prices and services vary from free online calculators to companies with live financial advisers who will file your Social Security application, monitor your account and provide you with a social security optimization report.

Chapter 6: The File and Suspend Approach to Maximizing Benefits (The "62 / 70 Split")

The "File and Suspend" approach is frequently called the "62 / 70 Split" it is another way to boost benefits. The file and suspend methodology allows the spouse of the high earner to collect benefits while the high earner accrues DRCs. The file and suspend approach works best for couples that have a high earner and a spouse that has never worked (or is a very low earner). The FRA high earner spouse files for benefits and immediately suspends his or her application. This allows the low earner to file for spousal benefits. Often the low earner is 62. The high earner continues to work, accrues DRCs, and retires at 70 (the 62 / 70 split). If the FRA high earner so desires he or she can "claw back" to the date he or she originally suspended their application and collect "back pay". In this situation, the big paycheck is nice but it is offset by a reduction in the amount of DRCs. There is an alternative option to the File and Suspend approach that is called the File and Suspend Combo Strategy. In this situation the FRA high earner files and suspends. The FRA low earner spouse files a "Restricted Application" for spousal benefits only and continues to work. At 70 the high earner re-applies for benefits and receives his or her DRCs. At 70 the low earner spouse switches from spousal benefits to claim his or her own benefits (which include four-years of DRCs). In other words, at 70 both spouses claim their own benefits that each benefit includes four years of DRCs.

Chapter 7: How Working After Retirement Can Increase Your Benefits

According to the SSA working after retirement will allow you to increase your monthly benefit in two ways. First, each year you work adds another year of earnings to your work record. Higher lifetime earnings may mean higher benefits when you retire. Second, each year you work after your FRA allows you to accrue Delayed Retirement Credits (DRCs). Currently DRCs increase you monthly benefit by 8 percent for each year you work after FRA. (However, keep in mind that if you delay retirement you should still enroll in Medicare at 65.) If you are an early retiree and work, the SSA will deduct $1 in benefits for every $2 earned over $14,640. In the year you turn FRA, the SSA will deduct $1 in every $3 earned above $38,880. If you are over FRA, you can earn as much as you like without any loss of benefits.

Chapter 8: What Could Reduce Your Benefits?

There are several ways that you can receive fewer benefits than what's stated on your Social Security Statement (www.ssa.gov/mystatement). For example your employer may have what's called an "integrated pension plan". Integrated pension plans include the amount paid by your employer to Social Security in your pension amount. The following is an example, let's say that your annual Social Security benefit is $8,000 (remember that over the years you paid half of the FICA taxes and your employer paid the other half.) Your annual pension from your employer is $10,000 per year. Your employer can cut $4,000 from your pension because it is "integrated" with Social Security. Therefore your annual adjusted pension would be $6,000 and your Social Security benefits would be $8,000 for a total of $14,000 per year in benefits. Additionally, the Government Pension Offset (GPO) provision reduces spousal and widow(er) Social Security benefits according to a pre-determined formula. For individuals who receive a large pension for work not covered by Social Security this generally means that they will not receive any spousal Social Security benefits. If you qualify for an "uncovered" pension and Social Security, the Windfall Elimination Provision (WEP) can reduce the amount of Social Security benefits you receive. One maximizing strategy for couples affected by WEP is for the high earner spouse to delay retirement and receive spousal benefits from the low earner spouses "un-covered" pension while the pension owner collects payments.

Chapter 9: Conclusion

The final chapter of the book includes how monitor changes in Social Security regulations and brief listing of additional sources of information.

CHAPTER 1: INCREASING YOUR BENEFITS BY SELECTING THE "RIGHT" APPLICATION DATE

Selecting the "Right Application Date" strategy to:
- ❖ maximize your Social Security Benefits.
- ❖ implement the best possible claiming plan for up to age 70.
- ❖ increase survivor benefits.
- ❖ reduce or avoid paying taxes on their Social Security benefits.

Social Security retirement benefits are playing a bigger role in people's lives than ever before. About 10,000 seniors in the U.S. will turn 66 every day over the next 20 years. Under current law, if you have average earnings, your Social Security retirement benefits should replace about 40 percent of your pre-retirement earnings. The percentage is lower for people in the upper income brackets and higher for people with low incomes.

It is not necessary to know all of the rules of Social Security. However, it is critical to understand the rules that are applicable to your unique earnings record and financial position. Understanding these rules will assist you to developing an optimal claiming strategy that can make the difference of living in near-poverty or enjoying the retirement lifestyle you expected.

Social Security Benefits are a Retiree's First Line of Defense

Knowing how much you can expect from Social Security and following a pre-determined claiming strategy to maximize your benefits can result in more money, security, and self-confidence in retirement. Finance professionals believe that Social Security benefits are a retiree's first line of defense against inflation and outliving savings. Social Security eliminates investment risk, provides inflation fighting increases and a life-long source of income. As employers move from defined benefit plans to defined contribution plans, such as 401(k)'s, individuals are now responsible for the investment risk that use to be the obligation of the employer. This has increased the value of Social Security benefits to retirees. (See the Glossary of Social Security terms at the back of this book for definitions of defined benefit and defined contribution retirement plans.)

Your "Red Zone" Years

Many finance professionals define the "Red Zone" as five years before retirement and five years after retirement. Decisions made during this ten-year period can have long-range consequences. Therefore, it is important to know about as many options as possible to make the financial decisions that are right for you and your family.

In my option, the most important Red Zone decision is when to claim Social Security benefits. Your life expectancy is an important factor in this decision. Social Security Administration (SSA) representatives have been trained to determine what the highest benefit a claimant can receive today. This point of view fails to take into consideration the increased longevity of most Americans.

According to the SSA, a man reaching 65 in 2012 can expect to live, on average, until 83. A woman turning 65 in 2012 can expect to live, on average, until 85. Additionally, about one out of every four 65-year olds today will live past 90 and one out of 10 will live past 95.

The SSA provides an online Life Expectancy Calculator that is useful for determining when you should apply for your Social Security Benefits. Remember, this online calculator does not take into consideration your current health, lifestyle, and family history which could increase or decrease your individual life expectancy. You'll find the SSA Life Expectancy Calculator at www.socialsecurity.gov/OACT/population/longevity.html.

Who is Eligible for Social Security Benefits?

Eligibility for Social Security benefits is based on income earned during your working years. The minimum age for working is 16 years. Minors younger than 16-years old need work permits. To get a Social Security card you'll need to prove U.S. Citizenship, Age and your Identity using any of the following documents:

❖ **U.S. Citizenship:** U.S. birth certificate or U.S. passport
❖ **Age:** Religious record before age 5, U.S. hospital record of birth, U.S. passport
❖ **Identity:** U.S. driver's license, state issued non-driver identification card, U.S. passport

Some documents, such as your U.S. passport, can be used for several requirements. All documents must be originals or certified copies by the issuing agency. Next complete the Social Security Administration form SS-5 (located at www.ssa.gov/online/ss-5.pdf/).

If you live or receive mail in Bronx, NY, Brooklyn, NY, Queens, NY, Orlando, FL (Orange, Osceola and Seminole counties), Sacramento County, CA, Phoenix, AZ (Maricopa County and Apache Junction Area), Las Vegas, NV, Philadelphia, PA or Greater Twin Cities Metropolitan Area, MN you must apply in person or by mail to a Social Security Card center for an original or replacement Social Security card. If you do not live in these areas, you can mail or take your Social Security card application and original documentation to your local Social Security office. However, if you are age 12 or older and have never received a Social Security number, you must apply in person. To find your local Social Security offices enter your zip code positioned at the bottom of the SSA Locator Page at www.socialsecurity.gov/locator.

Replacement Social Security Cards and Changing Information on Your Social Security Record

Getting a copy of your Social Security card or correcting SSA information uses the same form. If your name, citizenship or birthdate needs to be corrected on your Social Security record download, follow instructions and complete the Application for a Social Security Card Form located at www.socialsecurity.gov/online/ss-5.pdf. (You may receive three replacement Social Security cards per calendar year and 10 replacement Social Security cards in a lifetime.) The Application for a Social Security Card Form is used for applications for an original Social Security card, to apply for a replacement Social Security card, and to change or correct information on you Social Security number record.

If you are uncertain that your work is "covered" by Social Security ask yourself the following questions:
1. Were you asked to provide your Social Security number for the job?
2. Did you fill out a W-4 form for federal and state withholding taxes?
3. Did you receive a W-2 statement from your employer at the end of the calendar year for your earnings?

The Social Security Credit System

The year of your birth affects the number of credits needed to be eligible to receive Social Security benefits.
- ❖ Individuals born before 1929 need three credits per year. For example, if you were born in 1928 you only need 39 work credits; if you were born in 1927 you need 38 work credits to be eligible for Social Security retirement benefits.
- ❖ Individuals born after 1929 need a least 40 credits (10 years) to be eligible for Social Security benefits.
- ❖ If a worker dies before full retirement age (FRA), the deceased earning's record will require less work credits to qualify for survivors

benefits. (You'll find more information about this subject in Chapter 3: Optimal Claiming Strategies for Widow(er)s and Survivors.)

The SSA uses a credit system and the amount you earned to determine eligibility. In 2012 to earn one credit, a worker must earn income, on which Social Security is paid, of at least $1,130. This is defined as "covered" income. ("Uncovered" earnings are income that a worker does not pay FICA taxes on.) A work year is divided into four quarters; a quarter equals a three-month period. A worker can earn a maximum of 4 credits (quarters) per year.

Additionally, the Social Security Administration (SSA) takes into account how much you earn when calculating credits.

For example, if you earn at least $4,520 in January and February of 2012 and don't work for the rest of the year. The SSA with credit your account with 4 credits ($4,520 / $1,130 = 4).

It is important to understand that during your work history, you may have held an uncovered job or completed service that is not considered to be included in determining eligibility for SSA benefits. Examples of these jobs include:

❖ Railroad employees with more than 10 years of service.
❖ Employees of some state and local governments that chose not to participate in Social Security.
❖ Children younger than age 21 who do household chores for a parent (except a child age 18 or older who works in the parent's business).

"Uncovered" employment was also affected by the Civil Service Retirement Act, which became effective on August 1, 1920, which established a retirement system for certain Federal employees. It was replaced by the Federal Employees Retirement System (FERS) for Federal employees who first entered covered service on and after January 1, 1987. www.opm.gov/retire/pre/csrs/index.asp/.

Getting Credit for Military Service

According to the SSA there are usually no restrictions on claiming both social security benefits and military service retirement benefits. You will get your full Social Security benefit based on your earnings.

You do not need to take any action before applying for your Social Security benefits. However, you may be asked to provide proof of military service at that time. Earnings for active military service or active duty training have been covered under Social Security since 1957. The SSA covers inactive duty in the armed forces reserves (such as weekend drills) since 1988.

If you Served in the Military Before 1957

If you served in the military before 1957, you did not pay Social Security taxes, the SSA gave you special credit for some of your service. See the SSA publication located at www.ssa.gov/pubs/10017.html for details.

Downloading your Individual Social Security Statement

If you do not know or are uncertain about the number of credits you have acquired on your earnings record, you can check your individual Social Security Statement. For your convenience, you can download the Social Security Statement at www.ssa.gov/mystatement.

As of May 2011 the SSA stopped automatically mailing personal benefit statements to individuals under the age of 60. Individuals under 60 who want paper statements have to request mailed copies of their annual statements. Personal Social Security statements include:

- ❖ Estimates of retirement benefits you may receive at specific ages
- ❖ Approximations of disability benefits
- ❖ Your earnings record
- ❖ Assessments of retirement or survivor family benefits
- ❖ Information about how to enroll in Medicare
- ❖ Estimates of how much you have paid in Social Security and Medicare taxes
- ❖ Suggestions for what to consider if you plan to retire at age 55 or older
- ❖ General SSA information

As of this date, you can download your personal statement by creating a *My* Social Security account at www.ssa.gov/mystatement. You will asked to provide some personal information, then you can create a user ID and password. Once you have a *My* Social Security account you will be able to view or download your statement at any time. Additionally, the Web site offers an example of a statement at www.ssa.gov/mystatement/SSA-7005-OL.pdf. You may want to compare your personal Social Security statement with the example SSA statement to determine if there are any errors.

Table 1.1 Example of Individual Social Security Statement

Your Estimated Benefits

*Retirement   You have earned enough credits to qualify for benefits. At your current earnings rate, if you continue
working until...
your full retirement age (66 years), your payment would be about .... $ 1,506 a month
age 70, your payment would be about .... $ 1,988 a month
age 63, your payment would be about .... $ 1,264 a month

*Disability   You have earned enough credits to qualify for benefits. If you became disabled right now
your payment would be about... $ 1,506 a month

*Family   If you get retirement or disability benefits, your spouse and children also may qualify for benefits.
*Survivors   You have earned enough credits for your family to receive survivors benefits. If you die this year,
certain members of your family may qualify for the following benefits:
Your child.. $ 1,130 a month
Your spouse who is caring for your child.. $ 1,130 a month
Your spouse, if benefits start at full retirement age .... $ 1,506 a month
Total family benefits cannot be more than.. $ 2,796 a month
Your spouse or minor child may be eligible for a special one-time death benefit of $255.

SOURCE: Social Security Administration, (www.ssa.gov), 2012.

Table 1.1 is an example of a Social Security Statement. The first sentence indicates that the individual has earned enough work credits to qualify for retirement benefits. The FRA for the individual described in Table 1.1 is age 66. If this individual continues to have earnings at the current rate the estimated FRA retirement benefit is $1,506. Early retirement at age 63 is about $1,264 and retirement at age 70 is around $1,988. (The statement in Table 1.1 is for someone who is 63 years old. Early retirement at age 62 is possible.)

Table 1.1 is useful for planning purposes. For example, it is likely that the spousal benefit will be less than the individual's FRA benefit of $1,506. The statement in Table 1.1 points to useful Social Security publications about the Windfall Elimination Provision (WEP) and Government Pension Offset (GPO) which are discussed in Chapter 8: What Could Reduce Your Benefits?

Making Corrections to your Earning's Record

After reviewing your individual Social Security statement (www.ssa.gov/mystatement) if you discover an error or if earnings are missing from your work record, you should find proof of what needs to be corrected. An error may be due to the wrong Social Security number being recorded. This error may be an employer error or you may have made the mistake about the name and Social Security number you used when you worked. You have three-years and 15 days to make a correction to your SSA statement. The SSA considers the following proof:

❖ A W-2 form (Wage and Tax Statement)
❖ A tax return
❖ A wage stub or pay slip
❖ Your own wage records
❖ Any other written documents showing that you worked.

If the error concerns your earnings with your current employer, contact the Payroll Department and ask them to verify your earnings. Ask the Human Resources department to provide you with written verification of the details of your job appointment. The job appointment verification should include the needed correct information.

If the error was with a previous employer, the previous Human Resources Department may have a record of your job appointment and earnings.

If the business no longer exists or if the earnings were from self-employment try to locate your own records. If you cannot find any written documents that show your earnings, try to remember the following facts and write them down:

❖ Where you worked
❖ The name of your employer
❖ The dates you worked
❖ How much you earned

After you have gathered your documents or have made a list of all of the information you can remember, contact Social Security. The SSA will work with you to correct your earnings record. This could take some time. Therefore it is important to review your earning record at least once a year. To sum it up, to make corrections to earnings contact Social Security, make copies of the information you are sending for the correction and complete the form at www.ssa.gov/online/ssa-7008.pdf .

When Should You Start Social Security Retirement Benefits?

As stated in this book's introduction, according to the Social Security Administration (SSA) in 2009, 72 percent of the 2.7million new filers claimed Social Security retirement benefits early. Many of these individuals continue to work after claiming Social Security retirement benefits and paid taxes on the benefits they received.

Table 1.2 shows examples of someone claiming benefits before a Full Retirement Age (FRA) of 66 and a monthly benefit of $1,000. If the applicant claims benefits at 62 he or she will receive $750 per month (a permanent 25 percent reduction). If the applicant claims benefits at full retirement age he or she will receive $1,000 per month. If the applicant was born between 1943 and 1954 (see Table 1.4 for details) and waits until he or she is 70, the monthly benefit will permanently increase by 32 percent. The 32 percent increase is Delayed Retirement Credits (DRCs) of 8 percent per year.

Table 1.2 How Application Dates Change Monthly Benefit Amounts

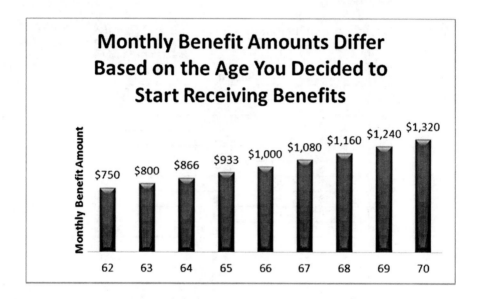

SOURCE: Social Security Administration (www.ssa.gov), 2012.

What are the Maximum Social Security Retirement Benefits?

In 2012 the maximum monthly benefit at 66 (full retirement age) is $2,012. The maximum for 62 year old retirees is $1,509 per month. In 2012, individuals who delayed retirement to age 70 can receive a maximum of $2,659 per month. Spouses cannot claim DRCs. Therefore the FRA spousal benefit is 50 percent of the earner's FRA benefit.

What are the Minimum Social Security Retirement Benefits?

"Special Minimum" benefits are payable to folks with long periods of relatively low earnings. To be eligible for special minimum benefits individuals must have at least 11 years of FICA covered earnings. For more about qualifying for Special Minimum benefits see www.ssa.gov/OACT/COLA/limitedapplic.html. Effective January 1979 special minimum benefits amounts were allowed to receive automatic Cost-Of-Living (COLA) increases. Table 1.3 illustrates the special minimum retirement benefit for the earner and minimum benefit for the worker's family as of December 2011. (For a definition of "Maximum Family Benefit" refer to Chapter 2: Increasing Your Benefits by Utilizing Spousal and Family Benefits, the section titled, "Family Benefits for your Spouse, Child and Dependent Parents".)

Table 1.3: Minimum Benefit Amount for Earner and Family

Number of Years of Coverage	Primary Insurance Amount	Maximum Family Benefit
11	$38.20	$58.10
12	$77.80	$117.70
13	$117.60	$177.10
14	$157.00	$236.30
15	$196.20	$295.40
16	$236.00	$355.10
17	$275.60	$414.90
18	$315.20	$474.00
19	$354.70	$533.50
20	$394.40	$592.50
21	$434.10	$652.40
22	$473.40	$711.70
23	$513.60	$771.90
24	$553.10	$830.80
25	$592.50	$889.60
26	$632.70	$950.10
27	$671.80	$1,009.30
28	$711.50	$1,068.50
29	$751.10	$1,128.30
30	$790.60	$1,187.00

SOURCE: Social Security Administration (www.ssa.gov), 2012.

How Longevity Affects When You Should Apply for Social Security

Based on mathematical models, William Reichenstein and William Meyer (2011) provide the following suggestions for the optimal age for claiming benefits based on longevity when an individual whose FRA is age 66 when:

❖ Life expectancy is less than 75 years: The best age for applying for benefits is age 62.

❖ Life expectancy is from 75 to less than 77 years old: The maximum cumulative benefits will be achieved if the individual applies at age 64.

❖ Life expectancy is from 77 to less than 80 years old: Reichenstein and Meyer suggest that if someone retires at 66 or 67 their "break-even" age is 79.5 years. Therefore if life expectancy is 77 to 80 years, the individual should apply for benefits at age 67.

❖ Life expectancy is from 80 to less than 83 years old: The optimal age for applying for benefits is age 69.

❖ Life expectancy is 83 years old or greater: Individuals should delay applying for benefits until age 70.

If you like to complete online questionnaires, you'll enjoy The Living to 100 Life Expectancy Calculator located at www.livingto100.com. This online questionnaire is more comprehensive than the one located at the SSA Web site (www.socialsecurity.gov/OACT/population/longevity.html). Take the quiz to find an individualized estimate of your life expectancy.

According to The Living to 100 Life Expectancy Calculator elements that can affect your longevity include:

1. **Your family genetics:** For example, do you have at least one relative that lived into their 90s?

2. **Medical:** Are you in good general health?

3. **Nutrition:** Do you regularly eat vegetables and salads?

4. **Lifestyle:** Do you smoke cigarettes, cigars or a pipe?

5. **Personal Situation:** Are you under stress?

How Early Retirement Reduces Benefits

As shown in Table 1.1 for the rest of their lives early retirement claimants will receive reduced benefits. In contrast, individuals who delay claiming Social Security benefits increase the amount of benefits they will receive.

Let's take someone born in 1942 as an example. Table 1.3 illustrates that if he (or she) retires at age 62 they will receive 75 5/6 percent of their full benefit amount. Retirement at age 66 results in receiving 101 ¼ percent of the total benefit. Retiring at age 70 results in receiving 131 ¼ percent of the total benefit amount. To sum it up, in this example, each year of delay receives a 7 ½ percent increase in the monthly payment amount. Therefore, the simplest strategy for maximizing your Social Security benefit is to delay applying for Social Security for as long as possible.

Getting Official Documents for When You Apply for Benefits

When you apply for Social Security benefits you'll need your birth certificate for retirement benefits, and marriage, divorce and death records for spousal, ex-spousal, survivor or dependent benefits. The Centers for Disease Control and Prevention (CDC) provide a helpful Web page located at www.cdc.gov/nchs/w2w.htm that offers links to where to write for vital records.

Select the correct state and area and follow the provided guidelines at www.cdc.gov/nchs/w2w/guidelines.htm. The Federal government does not provide certificates for benefits. For your information, many states will allow you to order via telephone, online or by mail. Charges for each certificate vary but average around $20 each. Allow two to three weeks for delivery. However, for an extra change many states have overnight express mail.

Table 1.1 indicates that all workers can retire at age 62 and receive benefits. It doesn't matter what the worker's full retirement age (FRA) is. Additionally, all workers can retire anytime between age 62 and 70. The following example shows how the earlier you retire the more your benefits are reduced.

Paul was born in 1939 and decides to retire on his 62nd birthday. Full retirement benefits would be $2,000 per month at age 65 and 4 months (see Table 1.4). The following shows how to calculate Paul's early retirement benefits.

1. Paul is retiring 40 months early.
2. The monthly benefit reduction percentage is 1/180 for the first 36 months (1/180 X 36 = 20%)
3. The monthly benefit reduction for the four subsequent months is 1/240 per month (1/240 X 4 = 1.6668%)

4. The total permanent reduction to Paul's benefits is 20% + 1.6668% = 21.6668%
5. The FRA benefit is multiplied by the reduction amount ($2,000 X 21.6668% = $433.34
6. Paul's monthly early benefit amount is $2,000 - $433.34 = **$1,566.60 (rounded)**.

Table 1.4 How Benefits Change Based on Date of Application

Year Of Birth	Full Retirement Age (FRA)	Credit for each year of delayed retirement after FRA (percent)	Benefit, as a Percentage of the Monthly Benefit, Beginning at Age...						
			62	63	64	65	66	67	70
1924	65	3	80	86 2/3	93 1/3	100	103	106	115
1925-26	65	3 1/2	80	86 2/3	93 1/3	100	103 1/2	107	117 1/2
1927-28	65	4	80	86 2/3	93 1/3	100	104	108	120
1929-30	65	4 1/2	80	86 2/3	93 1/3	100	104 1/2	109	122 1/2
1931-32	65	5	80	86 2/3	93 1/3	100	105	110	125
1933-34	65	5 1/2	80	86 2/3	93 1/3	100	105 1/2	111	127 1/2
1935-36	65	6	80	86 2/3	93 1/3	100	106	112	130
1937	65	6 1/2	80	86 2/3	93 1/3	100	106 1/2	113	132 1/2
1938	65, 2 mo.	6 1/2	79 1/6	85 5/9	92 2/9	98 8/9	105 5/12	111 11/12	131 5/12
1939	65, 4 mo.	7	78 1/3	84 4/9	91 1/9	97 7/9	104 2/3	111 2/3	132 2/3
1940	65, 6 mo.	7	77 1/2	83 1/3	90	96 2/3	103 1/2	110 1/2	131 1/2
1941	65, 8 mo.	7 1/2	76 2/3	82 2/9	88 8/9	95 5/9	102 1/2	110	132 1/2
1942	65, 10 mo.	7 1/2	75 5/6	81 1/9	87 7/9	94 4/9	101 1/4	108 3/4	131 1/4
1943-54	66	8	75	80	86 2/3	93 1/3	100	108	132
1955	66, 2 mo.	8	74 1/6	79 1/6	85 5/9	92 2/9	98 8/9	106 2/3	130 2/3
1956	66, 4 mo.	8	73 1/3	78 1/3	84 4/9	91 1/9	97 7/9	105 1/3	129 1/3
1957	66, 6 mo.	8	72 1/2	77 1/2	83 1/3	90	96 2/3	104	128
1958	66, 8 mo.	8	71 2/3	76 2/3	82 2/9	88 8/9	95 5/9	102 2/3	126 2/3
1959	66, 10 mo.	8	70 5/6	75 5/6	81 1/9	87 7/9	94 4/9	101 1/3	125 1/3
1960 and later	67	8	70	75	80	86 2/3	93 1/3	100	124

Note: Persons born on January 1 of any year should refer to the previous year of birth.
SOURCE: Social Security Administration (www.ssa.gov), 2012.

Let's assume that Paul decides to stay on the job until he is 64 and 6 months. The following example shows what his permanent monthly benefit will be without the annual Cost-Of-Living adjustments (COLAs).

1. Paul is retiring 10 months early.
2. The monthly benefit reduction percentage is 1/180 X 10 = 5.5556%
3. The FRA benefit is multiplied by the reduction amount ($2,000 X 5.556% = $111.12)
4. Paul's monthly benefit at age 64 and 6 months will be $2,000 - $111.12 = **$1,888.80 (rounded)**

The Cumulative Impact of Early Retirement

In our earlier example, Paul retired 10-months early and received a reduced benefit of about $1,888 per month versus a FRA benefit of $2,000 per month. This slight reduction may not seem like a lot of money at 64. However, Table 1.5 shows how these few dollars can add up over the years.

Table 1.5 The Cumulative Effects of Early Retirement

Comparison of Cumulative Benefits for Delayed, FRA and Early Retirement Benefits			
Age	Paul Delays Retirement to 70	Paul Retires at FRA	Paul Retires 10-Months Early
66	$0	$40,000	$56,400
70	$0	$136,000	$147,264
75	$159,200	$256,000	$260,544
80	$318,400	$376,000	$373,824
85	$477,600	$496,000	$487,104
90	$636,800	$616,000	$600,384
95	$796,000	$736,000	$713,664

Note: These payments do not include Cost-Of-Living Increases (COLAs).

Paul was born in 1939 so he receives a 7 percent increase to his FRA benefits for each year that he works over FRA (see Table 1.4 for details). If Paul retires at FRA then he receives his FRA benefit amount. If Paul retires early his monthly payment is permanently reduced.

There are many issues about early retirement and receiving a permanently reduced benefit. A decreased benefit affects the amount of the annual Cost-Of-Living Adjustment (COLA) increase. For example, if the COLA is 3 percent and the monthly benefit is $1,000, the amount of the COLA increase is $1,000 X .03 = $30 or $30. In contrast, someone with a $750 benefit would receive $22.50 ($750 X .03 = $22.50). The increased monthly payment amount becomes the new basis for the next COLA increase.

Calculating Annual Cost-Of-Living Increases (COLAs)

Claimants receive annual Cost-Of-Living increases based on the Consumer Price Index for Urban Wage Earners and Clerical Workers. COLAs ensure that benefits keep up with inflation. For more information see www.ssa.gov/OACT/STATS/cpiw.html.

Table 1.6 is a graphical representation of Table 1.5. Table 1.6 shows the long-term effects of retiring just 10-months early.

Table 1.6 Example of Delayed, FRA and Early Payments

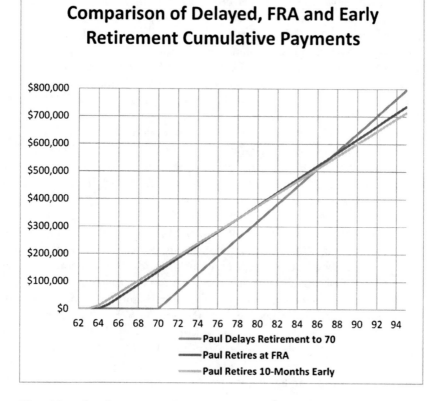

The delayed retirement option is the clear winner for highest cumulative payments. The break-even age for all three options is around age 86. After age 86 these payments have a greater value. As individuals get older inflation puts downward pressure on the purchasing power of savings. This increases the importance of each and every benefit dollar.

Early Retiree Calculation Assumptions

In one example of Paul we assume that he works until 62. If Paul stops work at age 58 then applies for early retirement benefits at age 62, on average the benefits will be reduced by $10 to $20 for each year of reduced or no earnings. This could result in benefits being $40 to $80 less per month.

Taxation of Social Security Retirement Benefits for Early Retirees

After claiming early benefits many individuals have discovered that they need to work. If you discover after retiring that you need to work (at age 62 through FRA) you may pay taxes on your benefits. In 2012 you can earn $14,640 and not pay taxes on your benefits. The SSA will deduct $1 for every $2 earned above $14, 600 until the beneficiary reaches full-retirement age. Beneficiaries that are full retirement age can earn $38,880 per year and not pay taxes on their benefits. The SSA will deduct $1 for every $3 earned above $38,880. Use the Internal Revenue Service (IRS) Notice 703, which is downloadable in PDF format at www.irs.gov/pub/irs-pdf/n703.pdf to determine if any of your benefits are taxable.

Other useful IRS publications for early retiree's include:

❖ Taxation of Social Security and Railroad Retirement Benefits. For details about the taxation of these benefits see IRS publication 915, Social *Security and Equivalent Railroad Retirement Benefits* which is available online in PDF format at www.irs.gov/pub/irs-pdf/p915.pdf .

❖ Information about the taxation of IRAs is available at www.irs.gov/pub/irs-pdf/p590.pdf in downloadable PDF format. This publication covers traditional and Roth IRAs and includes news about the 2011 and 2012 changes to both accounts.

❖ If you have or expect to receive pension or annuity income, discover in advance if it is taxable. IRS Publication 575, *Pension and Annuity Income* is free and downloadable in PDF format at www.irs.gov/pub/irs-pdf/p575.pdf.

Examples of Taxation on Early Retirement Benefits

Table 1.7 is a brief summary that shows three benefit amounts $700, $900 and $1,100. The second column shows three levels of earnings $14,600 or less (the current "tax-free" amount), $15,000 and $20,000. The third column shows reduced annual benefits due to earnings.

If you are an early retiree, the SSA will not reduce your benefits if your earn $14,600 or less. Let's say you have a benefit of $700 per month ($8,400 per year). If you are an early retiree and earn $20,000 per year, your annual benefits of will be reduced by $2,680 ($8,400 - $5,720 = $2,680) and you will receive $5,720 in benefits for the year. (For details refer to Table 1.7.)

Bottom line, there is a high penalty if you file for early retirement benefits and work. *On the other hand, if you are over FRA you can earn as much as you like and it doesn't affect your benefit amount.*

If you are uncertain about how much of your Social Security benefits you will lose due to taxes check with your financial adviser or CPA. For general guidance refer to the IRS Web site for Publication 554 (2011), Tax Guide for Seniors located at www.irs.gov/publications/p554/index.html.

Table 1.7 Early Retirement Benefit Reductions and Earnings Example

If your Monthly Social Security Benefit is	And you Earn	You will Receive Yearly Benefits of
$700	$14,640 or less	$8,400
$700	$15,000	$8,220
$700	20,000	$5,720
$900	$14,640 or less	$10,800
$900	$15,000	$10,620
$900	$20,000	$8,120
$1,100	$14,640 or less	$13,200
$1,100	$15,000	$13,020
$1,100	$20,000	$10,520

SOURCE: Social Security Administration (www.ssa.gov), 2012.

Definitions of Earned Income and Early Retirement Benefits

Earned income for Social Security purposes is similar to earned income previous to early retirement. For example, your wages count toward Social Security limits. For those self-employed only net earnings from self-employment are counted. While you are collecting early retirement Social Security benefits you can expect to pay FICA taxes on wages and taxes on pension or retirement plan contributions if the contribution amount is included in your gross wages.

The SSA provides this example, let's say that Mike's FRA benefits are $1,000. In 2012 Mike claims early retirement at age 62 and receives $750 per month in benefits. Mike returns to work and 12 months of benefits are withheld. The SSA would recalculate Mike's benefit at FRA and pay Mike $800 per month (in today's dollars).

The SSA goes on to provide a second scenario. Let's say that Mike earned so much between the ages of 62 and 66 that all benefits during *that time period are withheld. In that case, starting at age 66 Mike would be paid $1,000 per month in benefits.*

What's Not Included in Early Retirement "Earned Income"

Earnings (for the wage earner and the self-employed) are counted in the year the income is received. Additionally, the SSA reduces retirement benefits based on *earned income*. The good news is that money received from "special sources" before claiming early retirement benefits is not counted as earned income. Exempted income can include:

- ❖ Accumulated vacation pay or sick leave
- ❖ Accumulated commissions
- ❖ Bonuses
- ❖ Deferred compensation
- ❖ Private retirement fund payments
- ❖ Payments for completed self-employed work (with payments received more than one year after claiming early retirement benefits)

In conclusion, the SSA states that it is important to keep in mind that the Social Security Administration has no authority to withhold state or local taxes from your monthly benefits. *Many states and local authorities do not tax Social Security benefits. However, you should contact your state or local taxing authority for more information.*

Determining Your "Break-Even Age" if you Retire Early

Let's say that you decide to retire early. You want to know what the beak-even age is for taking reduced benefits over a longer period of time. Refer to your individual Social Security Statement for your estimated retirement benefits at the SSA Web site www.socialsecurity.gov/mystatement . (It takes less than five-minutes to set-up an account with your personalized User ID and Password.) Take special note of the FRA benefits and the early retirement benefits on the first page of your individual statement (for an example see Table 1.1). That's where you will find the information used in the following beak-even example.

Table 1.8 shows the break-even analysis for the following example. Let's say that Henry's FRA benefits are $1,506 per month (or $18,702 per year) and early retirement benefits at age 63 (Henry is older than 62) are $1,264 per month (or $15,168 per year). Henry wants to retire three (3) years early. What's Henry's estimated break-even age?

1. Calculate the savings needed to fund the delay if Henry retired at FRA by multiplying 3 X $18,702 = $56,106.
2. Calculate the number of years to break-even by using the following formula $56,106 / ($18,702-$15,168) = $56,106 /$3,534 = 15.88 years. (That's rounded to 16 years.)
3. The break-even age is **63 + 16 = 79.**

Table 1.8 and the calculation above (using current dollars which will be automatically adjusted for inflation in the future by the SSA) indicates the effects of longevity on early retirement. Until age 79 Henry will receive **more** benefits than if he retired at his FRA. After age 79 Henry will receive **less** than if he retired at FRA due to his early retirement.

Table 1.8: Example of Early Retirement Break-Even Analysis

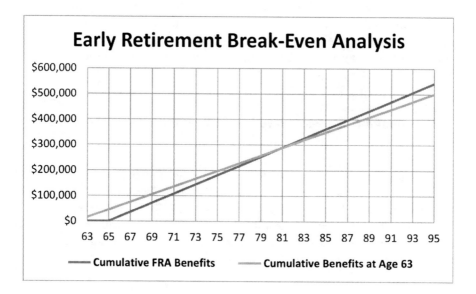

Early Retirement and how it Influences Your Spouse's Benefits

A lower-earning spouse that is at least 62 years old can claim Social Security benefits based on his (or her) own earnings record. For example, a spouse who has never worked can claim "spousal" benefits if the other spouse is claiming benefits or has claimed benefits and "suspended" the application (see Chapter 6: The "File and Suspend" Approach to Maximizing Benefits). If you decide to retire early, the amount of benefits your spouse is entitled to will be permanently reduced. Additionally, if a spouse is not FRA and wants to claim spousal benefits on the work record of an early retired spouse, things get complicated. That is, the earner's benefit is reduced for early retirement, and that benefit is reduced *again* if the earner's spouse retires early. See Chapter 2: Increasing Your Benefits by Utilizing Spousal Benefits for details.

Maximizing Your Benefits by Delaying Your Application

According to a *Kiplinger* article (Sheedy and Garland, April 2011) the following example was used to show the benefits of delaying claiming Social Security benefits. Sheedy and Garland state that delaying claiming Social Security benefits is comparable to a 62 year old applicant who would receive $1,125 a month in Social Security benefits if he claimed now and $1,980 a month if he claimed when he was 70. The monthly difference in income is $855. To receive an income of $855 per month our hypothetical retiree at 70 years old would have to purchase an immediate annuity for $116,600. Of course, the immediate annuity would not have a 100 percent survivor benefit or annual Cost-Of-Living adjustments (COLAs) to adjust for inflation. This comparison is one way to show the value of delaying claiming Social Security Benefits.

Important for Spouses: Delayed Retirement Credits (DRCs) and Your Spousal Benefit

Let's say that your spouse's FRA is 66 and his or her monthly benefit is $2,000. Your spouse decides to work until 70 and claims DRCs to increase his or her monthly benefit to $2,640 (see Table 1.4 for details). Your spousal benefit is still 50 percent of the FRA benefit of $2,000. In other words, the most you can receive as a spousal benefit is $1,000 per month. (There are different rules for widow(er)s or survivors.)

Delayed Retirement and How it Affects Your Benefits and Survivors

For an individual retiring at age 66 in 2012 the maximum benefit amount is $2,513. This figure is based on earning the maximum taxable amount for every year after age 21. If you decide to work full-time beyond your FRA you can increase your monthly benefit in three ways:

1. Each additional year of earnings is added to your work record. Higher lifetime earnings may result in higher benefits when you

retire. (For example, the FICA ceiling on earnings in 1960 was $4,800 compared to the FICA ceiling of $110,100 in 2012.)

2. Your benefit will increase by a certain percentage (see Table 1.9) each year if you delay retirement. These increases are called delayed retirement credits (DRCs) and are based on your year of birth. DRCs are automatically added from the time you reach FRA to when you start receiving benefits or reach 70.

3. If you die before reaching 70 years old, your spouse will still receive widow(er)'s or survivor's benefits that include your DRCs up to the month of your death.

Table 1.9 Delayed Retirement Credit by Year of Birth

Delayed Retirement Credit	
Year of Birth	Credit per Year
1917-24	3.00%
1925-26	3.50%
1927-28	4.00%
1929-30	4.50%
1931-32	5.00%
1933-34	5.50%
1935-36	6.00%
1937-38	6.50%
1939-40	7.00%
1941-42	7.50%
1943 and later	8.00%

SOURCE: Social Security Administration (www.ssa.gov), 2012.

Calculating the Attainment of Your Retirement Age

Table 1.9 shows how the SSA adds DRCs benefits based on your birthdate. However, the SSA has its own way of calculating time. The following are a few things you should know in advance:

1. Attaining your age the day before your birthday:
    a. If you are born on January 1 of a certain year. Your birth year is determined to be the previous year.
    b. Normally, benefits are calculated the first full-month after your 62nd birthday. Therefore if your birthday is October 25, your monthly benefits will start November 1.
    c. If your 62nd birthday is the first day or second day of the month, you are eligible the month of your 62nd birthday.

Therefore, if you turn 62 on October 1, your monthly benefits will start October 1.

d. Benefits for a certain month are generally paid the next month.

The Timing of Full Retirement Age (FRA)

As shown in Table 1.10 full retirement age (FRA) depends on the year of your birth. For most people it's between 65 and 66. When calculating your FRA a person born on January 1 of any year should refer to the normal retirement age for the previous year.

Table 1.10 Full Retirement Age (FRA) Varies

Normal Retirement Age	
Year of Birth	Age
1937 and prior	65
1938	65 and 2 months
1939	65 and 4 months
1940	65 and 6 months
1941	65 and 8 months
1942	65 and 10 months
1943-54	66
1955	66 and 2 months
1956	66 and 4 months
1957	66 and 6 months
1958	66 and 8 months
1959	66 and 10 months
1960 and later	67

SOURCE: Social Security Administration (www.ssa.gov), 2012.

The SSA provides a few examples of how the attainment of your retirement age can be computed and how FRA can impact your taxes:

Scenario #1: If you retire in the middle of a year, your earnings will be counted from January 1 (and not just from the date you retire).

Scenario #2: If you are under full retirement age for all of 2012, you are considered retired in any month your earnings are $1,220 or less and you did not perform substantial services in self-employment.

Scenario #3: For income tax purposes the SSA does not count income you earned beginning with the month you reached full retirement age.

Don't Forget to Enroll in Medicare Before You Turn 65 Years-Old

You don't have to be a Social Security benefit claimant to enroll and receive Medicare benefits. If you plan to take Medicare, you should sign up for the program three-months before your 65th birthday. (For many folks this is a year before FRA.) According to the SSA, if you don't sign up in a timely fashion you may encounter delays in receiving medical insurance, prescription drug coverage and you "could be charged higher premiums".

Day of the Month you can Expect to Receive Benefits

As stated earlier, Social Security benefits are paid the month after they are due. The benefit payment day is determined by the claimant's birthdate. For spousal benefits, the payment date is based on the birth date used for the spouse's work record. In contrast, if you and your spouse are claiming benefits on your own work record, you may receive two payments per month. For example, if you were born at the beginning of the month and your spouse was born at the end of the month there may be a two-week hiatus between payments. The following is the 2012 payment schedule:

- ❖ Benefits are paid on the second Wednesday for claimants with birth dates between the 1st and the 10th.
- ❖ Benefits are paid on the third Wednesday for claimants with birth dates between the 11th and 20th
- ❖ Benefits are paid on the third Wednesday for claimants with birth dates between the 21st and the 31st.

CHAPTER 2: INCREASING YOUR BENEFITS BY UTILIZING SPOUSAL AND FAMILY BENEFITS

Increasing monthly payments using spousal benefits work best for married couples:

- ❖ who have been married for at least ten years.
- ❖ whose age differences are greater than four years.
- ❖ who are both working.
- ❖ who have one low-earning and one high-earning spouse.
- ❖ who want to increase first death survivor benefits.

Utilizing spousal and family benefits is generally an easy way to boost Social Security benefits. Your spouse, ex-spouse, children, and dependent parents are entitled to benefits based on your work record. For example, even if your spouse has never worked or may be the "low earner" in your household he or she can claim benefits based on your work record. This chapter provides many of the details of how you or your spouse can take advantage of your marital and family relationships.

This chapter is followed by Chapter 3: Optimal Claiming Strategies for Widow(er) s and Survivors which takes this discussion one step further to discuss how the SSA rules change when a spouse, ex-spouse or other dependents become survivors.

For step-by-step directions and examples of specific claiming strategies for married couples to boost monthly benefits see Chapter 5: Maximizing Your Benefits by Claiming Now and Claiming More Later. Also see Chapter 6: The "File and Suspend" Approach to Maximizing Benefits.

The following shows how the SSA defines spouse and similar terms. As you may suspect the SSA has its own definitions.

Definitions of Spouse, Common-Law-Spouse, Ex-Spouse and Widow(er)

The following is a short list of how the SSA defines a spouse.

- ❖ **Spouse:** You are the spouse of the worker if, when he or she applied for benefits (1) you and the worker were married, or (2) you would have the status of a husband or a wife for that person's personal property if they had no will, or (3) you went through a marriage ceremony in good faith, which would have been valid except for a legal impediment.

❖ **Common-Law Spouse:** Social Security follows the laws of the state where the worker was residing at the time of death or the place where the worker was residing when the spouse applied for Social Security benefits. For a common-law marriage to be valid, it must have been contracted in a state where common-law marriages are recognized. (Many states do not honor common-law marriages, check with local laws.) Most states (even those in which a man and a woman could not enter into a valid common-law marriage) will generally recognize a common-law marriage validly entered into in another state. Again, check with local laws.

❖ **Same-Sex Spouse:** According to the Social Security Handbook, same sex couples are not considered spouses for SSA benefits. For example, under the Federal Defense of Marriage Act, an individual whose claim for benefits is based on a State recognized same-sex marriage or having the same status as spouse for State inheritance purposes cannot meet the statutory gender-based definition of widow or widower of the worker, including one who is divorced. Therefore, for all benefit purposes, the Social Security Administration does not recognize such an individual as the widow or widower of the deceased worker.

Ex-Spouse: If you are divorced and your marriage lasted 10 years or longer, you may receive benefits on your ex-spouse's record (even if he or she has remarried) if (1) you are unmarried, (2) you are age 62 or older; (3) your ex-spouse is entitled to Social Security retirement benefits, and (4) your ex-spouse's benefit that you are entitled to receive is more than the benefit you would receive based on your own work record. It is important to keep in mind that you do not need to contact or ask your ex-spouse for permission to apply for these benefits. Additionally:

o If your ex-spouse has **not** applied for retirement benefits, but can qualify for them, you can receive benefits on his or her record if you have been divorced for at least two years.

o If you meet the ex-spousal requirement for benefits and your ex-spouse dies, you automatically qualify for widow(er) benefits.

o If you remarry, you generally cannot collect benefits on your former spouse's record unless your later marriage ends (whether by death, divorce or annulment).

Unsure of Your Spousal Status?

If you have any questions about your status as a spouse or if you need documentation to support your spousal status, you should contact your Social Security Administration representative for clarification, verification, and assistance to support your spousal claim.

Family Benefits for your Spouse, Child and Dependent Parents

If you are getting Social Security retirement benefits, some members of your family can also receive benefits. In general, the Maximum Family Benefit amount is 150 to180 percent of the worker's benefit amount. Each family member is entitled to a monthly benefit. If benefits exceed the family maximum, the worker's benefit amount is not reduced. However, the benefit of other family members will be reduced (with the exception of an ex-spouse). Family members that are eligible for benefits include:

❖ Spouses who are age 62 or older
❖ Spouses who are younger than 62 (even if they have remarried), if they are taking care of a child entitled on your record who is younger than age 16 or disabled (for details on "entitled children" and "entitled disabled children" see below.)
❖ Former spouses, if they are age 62 or older
❖ Entitled children who are the earner's natural or legally adopted children up to age 18, or up to 19 if they are full-time students who have not yet graduated from high school
❖ Entitled disabled children under the age of 18 or 19 if in high school full-time, unmarried children 18 or older if disabled prior to age 22.
❖ Dependent parents (The earner's parents who receive 50 percent of more of their income from the worker.)

Note: More definitions of family members are included later in this chapter.

Spousal and Ex-Spousal Benefit Amounts

The SSA pays benefits to more individuals than the worker. It is important to note that payments to spouses and ex-spouses do not diminish the earner's benefits. (For example, the SSA will allow up to five spouses and ex-spouses can claim benefits on the earner's work record.) The following is a summary of the amount and eligibility requirements to receive benefits.

Spouse

❖ FRA or older can receive 50 percent of the worker's full payment amount

❖ Age 62 (assuming FRA of 66) can receive 35 percent of the worker's full payment amount

❖ Any age, while caring for the worker's entitled child can receive 50 percent the worker's full payment amount

Requirements:

- Worker must be receiving SSA benefits
- Claimant must be 62 or older, or caring for the worker's entitled child

Ex-Spouse

❖ FRA or older can receive 50 percent of the worker's full payment amount

❖ Age 62 (assuming FRA of 66) can receive 35 percent of the worker's full payment amount

Requirements:

- Worker must be age 62 or greater
- Worker may or may not have claimed Social Security Benefits
- Marriage existed for a minimum of 10 years
- Ex-spouse claimant must be 62
- Ex-spouse claimant is currently unmarried, or has remarried after age 60. (The ex-spouse cannot claim benefits from his or her former spouse and the current spouse at the same time.)

A Word about Taxes on Survivor and Disability Benefits

Widow(er) or survivor, and disability Social Security benefits are subject to the same tax rules as Social Security retirement benefits. To get more information about the taxability of survivor and disability Social Security payments refer to IRS Publication 915 "Social Security and Equivalent Railroad Retirement Benefits" located online at www.irs.gov/pub/irs-pdf/p915.pdf. IRS Publication 915 provides several examples with worksheets to illustrate how 2011 taxes are determined for individuals in different personal financial situations.

Retirees and Eligible Children

Many retirees have "second families" that include children that are eligible for Social Security benefits when their father or mother retires. To receive benefits the child must be your biological child, adopted child or step-child. A dependent grandchild is also eligible.

Requirements:

- ❖ Younger than 18 years old
- ❖ Between the ages of 18 and 19, but in elementary or secondary school full-time
- ❖ A full-time student (no higher than grade 12) or;
- ❖ Age 18 or older and severely disabled (the disability must have started before age 22.)

Subject to the limits of the Family Maximum Benefit amount (discussed in detail later in this chapter) each month an eligible child may receive up to 50 percent of the retiree's monthly benefit amount.

Benefits for Dependent Parents

A dependent parent is defined as the natural parent, or someone who became the earner's step-parent or adopting parent before the worker reached age 16. To be a dependent parent, the parent must be at least 62 years old and receive no less than 50 percent of his or her income from the earner before the earner died (or became disabled). The amount of the earner's benefit that eligible dependent parents are entitled to is as follows:

- ❖ One surviving parent -- 82½ percent.
- ❖ Two surviving parents -- 75 percent to each parent.

Jackie's parents are both over 62 years old. They are divorced and each lives alone. Jackie's parents both receive small Social Security benefits amounts but Jackie provides more than 50 percent of each parent's income. Jackie dies in an airplane crash. Jackie's full payment amount is $2,000. Therefore each dependent parent can receive 75 percent ($1,500) of Jackie's full payment (if this amount does not exceed the Family Maximum Benefit amount.)

Benefits for Dependent Children of Grandparents

According to the SSA a dependent grandchild or step-child may receive benefits on the earnings record of a grandparent or step-grandparent if the grandchild's natural or adoptive parents are deceased or disabled (1) at the time the grandparent became entitled to retirement or disability insurance benefits or died; or (2) at the beginning of the grandparent's period of disability which continued until he or she became entitled to disability or retirement insurance benefits or died. The SSA goes on to state that additional requirements include:

* ❖ The grandchild was legally adopted by the grandparent's surviving spouse in an adoption decreed by a court of competent jurisdiction within the United States.
* ❖ The grandchild's natural or adopting parent or stepparent must not have been living in the same household and making regular contributions to the child's support at the time the grandparent died.
* ❖ The grandchild must have lived with the grandparent in the United States before reaching age 18 and received at least one-half of his or her support from the grandparent for the year before the month the grandparent began receiving retirement or disability benefits or died.

Calculating the Family Maximum Benefit Amount

For the family of a worker who becomes 62 or dies in 2012 before attaining age 62 the Family Maximum Benefit (FMB) amount doesn't exceed the following formula:
1. 150% of the first $980 of the worker's benefit, plus
2. 272% of the worker's benefit over $980 through $1,415, plus
3. 134% of the worker's benefit over $1,415 through $1,845, plus
4. 175% of the worker's benefit over $1,845
5. Add amounts
6. Round to the lower multiple of $0.10

Let's say that a worker is 62 years old with a benefit of $1,800. The FMB is calculated as follows:
1. 150% X $980 = 1.5 X $980 = $1,470.00
2. 272% X ($1,415 - $980) = 2.72 X $435 = $1,183.20
3. 134% X ($1,845-$1,415) = 1.34 X $430 = $576.20
4. 175% X ($1,800 - $1845) = 1.75 X 0 = $0
5. Add amounts ($1,470.00 + $1,183.20 + $576.20 + $0) = $3,229.40
6. Rounded to lower multiple of $0.10 = **$3,229.40**

The Family Maximum Benefit is $3,229.40 or 179 percent of the worker's benefit. (There is a separate Family Maximum Benefit for Disability benefits.)

Family maximum rules do not apply to ex-spouses and are not included in the Family Maximum Benefit amount. In other words, the fact that an ex-spouse receives a benefit based on the earner's work record will not reduce the benefits of the earner's current family.

Distribution Adjustments Based on the Family Maximum Benefit

In some situations the number of dependents claiming benefits on an earner's record exceeds the FMB amount. For example, in Table 2.1 the earner's full benefit amount is $300.60 and the FMB is $535.10. Therefore the earner's dependents will have to divide $234.50 evenly between themselves. Note: The ex-spouse is not included in the FMB calculation and receives 50 percent of the earner's benefit ($150.30).

Table 2.1 Adjustments for Family Maximum Benefits (FMB)

Beneficiary	Original Benefit	Adjusted for the Maximum	Adjustment When Benefits not Payable to One Child	Adjustment When Benefits not Payable to Two Children
Insured person	$300.60	$300.60	$300.60	$300.60
Spouse	$150.30	$58.60	$78.10	$117.20
First child	$150.30	$58.60	$78.10	$117.20
Second child	$150.30	$58.60	$78.10	$0.00
Third child	$150.30	$58.60	$0.00	$0.00
Total	$901.80	$535.00	$534.90	$535.00

SOURCE: Social Security Administration (www.ssa.gov), 2012.

Table 2.1 illustrates how the earner's benefit is not reduced due to others claiming benefits on his or her work record. The second column shows the initial entitlement of each family member. The third column of Table 2.1 shows the redistribution of benefits due to the Family Maximum benefit calculation. The fourth column shows the readjustment when benefits are not paid to one child. The last column illustrates the readjustment when benefits are not paid to two children.

Family Members can be Entitled to More Than One Benefit

Dual Entitlement: Spouses and ex-spouses can be eligible for benefits in several ways. First, the spouse can claim benefits on his or her own work record. Second, the spouse or ex-spouse can claim benefits on the larger earning spouse's record. The two options are called "Dual Entitlement". The Dual Entitlement Provision states that if the spouse or ex-spouse is under FRA he or she will be paid benefits on his or her own work record first. If the under FRA spouse's benefits are higher than his or her spousal benefit, then the under FRA spouse would draw benefits from their own work record. *This reduced amount would be permanently locked in.*

On the other hand, if the spouse or ex-spouse is over FRA then he or she can claim spousal benefits only and can continue working to accrue Delayed Retirement Credits (DRCs). This would allow the over FRA spouse to change accounts and claim benefits increased by DRCs on his or her own account. (This is called a restricted application and it is discussed in detail in Chapter 5: Maximizing Your Benefits by Claiming Now and Claiming More Later.)

Entitlement to More Than One Benefit: The following is a quote from the Social Security Handbook, "If you are entitled to more than one benefit, only the higher benefit is payable, unless one of the benefits is either: (1) a retirement or disability insurance benefit or (2) both benefits are child's insurance benefits."

❖ **Exception #1 Retirement benefits:** According to the SSA it is possible to be entitled to a retirement (or disability) benefit as well as another higher benefit. In this case, the claimant will receive the retirement (or disability insurance benefit) plus the difference between this benefit and the higher one. If the higher benefit is not payable, either in whole or in part for one or more months, the retirement or disability insurance benefit may be payable.

Joan is entitled to retirement insurance benefits of $1,200 and to spousal benefits of $1,500. The total benefit payable to her is $1,500 made up of a retirement insurance benefit of $1,200 and a spousal benefit of $300. If the spousal benefit is not payable for some months because of her husband's earnings, she will receive her own retirement insurance benefit of $1,200.

❖ **Exception #2 Children's insurance benefits:** In general, when a claimant is entitled to several benefits, the SSA only pays the highest benefit. In some cases, a child may be entitled to benefits from the earning's record for a *higher* benefit, and to *lower* benefits on the lesser earnings record if certain conditions are met:

- o The benefit on that earner's record, before reduction for the Family Maximum Benefit (FMB) is higher, and
- o No other beneficiaries, who are entitled to any earning's record involved, would get a lower benefit than he or she would otherwise receive. In other words, receipt of the benefit would not lessen the amount received by another family member.

Adoption, Remarriage, and Family Maximum Benefits

Let's say that several years ago one of the parents of an adopted child died. The surviving spouse decides to remarry and the new spouse plans to adopt the child. The child is currently receiving survivor benefits. The adoption of a child already entitled to survivor benefits will not terminate the child's benefits.

How Selecting the Right Application Date Affects Your Spousal Benefits

How the SSA calculates spousal benefits appears to be complicated. According to the SSA, a married couple's lifetime earnings are calculated "independently" to determine the benefit amount for each spouse. Therefore each spouse receives a monthly benefit amount based on his or her own earnings. However, if one member of the couple earned low wages or did not earn the required number of Social Security credits to receive Social Security retirement benefits, that member of the couple may be eligible to receive benefits as a spouse.

In other words, the SSA always determines a benefit amount, independently of a spousal benefit amount. Then the SSA pays the spouse the higher amount. (It is important to point out that the worker always receives his or her full benefit amount. That is, the payment of spousal and ex-spousal benefits does not affect the benefit amount received by the worker.) The following example illustrates how this works.

Diana worked before her marriage and is entitled to a benefit of $400 per month on her own earning's record. Diana's FRA is 66 and she claims spousal benefits of 50 percent of her husband's monthly FRA benefit of $2,000. In other words, Diana's spousal benefit is $1,000.

(Diana can claim benefits of $400 per month on her own work record and receive less than her spousal benefit.) When Diana files for spousal benefits, the SSA will pay Diana $400 per month on her own work record and $600 per month in spousal benefits for a total spousal benefit of $1,000.

Calculating the Benefit Amount for Ex-Spouses

The SSA is generous with ex-spouses. It understands that a former spouse has no control over the actions of an ex-spouse (especially if a spouse decides to never retire and blocks an ex-spouse from claiming benefits on an earner's record). In 1985 the SSA made an exception to the rules. Such that qualified ex-spouses can file for spousal benefits at 62, even if the worker has not claimed his or her own benefits. This contrasts with the rules for the current spouse who has to wait until the worker files for benefits. This allows the ex-spouse to claim his or her own benefits and the reduced spousal benefits. Additionally, an ex-spouse who was married for ten-years each to several husbands can choose which husband's work record to claim ex-spousal benefits on. This option is another option not available to current spouses.

Showing an awareness of human behavior, the SSA has dampened the rush to divorce that these opportunities may encourage by requiring the ex-spouse to be divorced for two years before taking advantage of these options.

Claiming Benefits on an Estranged Ex-Spouses Earning's Records

If you meet the eligibility requirements for ex-spousal benefits, you do not need permission from your ex-spouse to claim these benefits. Additionally, the SSA will not mail a notice to your ex-spouse that you are claiming benefits. To apply for benefits on your ex-spouses earning's record you will need to know his or her Social Security number. If you do not have this information, provide his or her date and place of birth and the names of his or her parents. You can apply online, at your local SSA office or via telephone by calling 800-772-1213. For more information visit the SSA Web site and download a publication titled, "What Every Woman Should Know" at www.ssa.gov/pubs/10127.html#a0=14 .

Calculating Early Spousal Benefits

In general, spousal and ex-spousal benefits are automatically 50 percent of the primary worker's benefit. Spousal benefits are based on the worker's FRA benefit amount and the spouse's age. *Sometimes the spousal benefit is determined by the worker's FRA benefit even if the worker is receiving a different benefit amount.*

As shown in Table 2.2 individuals born from 1943 to 1954 and retiring at age 62 can expect their monthly Social Security benefits to be permanently reduced by 25 percent. If the spouse of an early retiree wants to retire early, his or her benefit amount is permanently reduced.

As a general rule, the earlier a spouse retires, the less the spouse will receive as a percentage of the working spouse's benefit. The following shows how the reduction is calculated:

❖ The spousal benefit is reduced 25/36 of one percent for each month an individual retires before FRA, up to 36 months.
❖ If the number of months is greater than 36 then the benefit is reduced by 5/12 of one percent per month.

The following are three scenarios using information from Table 2.2 that illustrate different ways that spousal benefits are reduced for early retirement.

Scenario #1 Early Spousal Payment when the Spouse Retires Early

The spousal benefit is reduced 25/36 of one percent for each month an individual retires before FRA, up to 36 months. If the number of months is greater than 36 then the benefit is reduced by 5/12 of one percent per month.

❖ Let's say that Jane wants to retire at age 62 and is 48 months from FRA. The worker's primary insurance amount is $1,500 per month due to early retirement. Therefore the 50 percent spousal benefit is $1,500 X 50% = $750 at FRA.
❖ Jane wants to receive benefits 48 months before FRA.
   o The reduction amount is 36 X 25/36 of one percent = 25 percent.
   o The reduction amount is 12 X 5/12 of one percent = 5 percent.
❖ The reduced spousal payment is $750 X 30 percent =$225.
❖ The monthly benefit amount is $750 - $225 = $525.

Scenario #2 Early Spousal Payments when Spouse Retires at FRA

The spousal benefit is reduced 25/36 of one percent for each month an individual retires before FRA, up to 36 months. If the number of months is greater than 36 then the benefit is reduced by 5/12 of one percent per month.

❖ Let's say that Jane wants to retire at age 62 and is 48 months from FRA. The worker's primary insurance amount is $2,000 per month. Therefore the 50 percent spousal benefit is $2.000 X 50% = $1,000 at FRA.

❖ Jane wants to receive benefits 48 months before FRA.
  o The reduction amount is 36 X 25/36 of one percent = 25 percent.
  o The reduction amount is 12 X 5/12 of one percent = 5 percent.

❖ The reduced spousal payment is $1,000 X 30 percent =$300.

❖ The monthly benefit amount is $1,000 - $300 = $700.

Scenario #3 Early Spousal Payments when Spouse Delays Retirement

The spousal benefit is reduced 25/36 of one percent for each month an individual retires before FRA, up to 36 months. If the number of months is greater than 36 then the benefit is reduced by 5/12 of one percent per month.

❖ Let's say that Jane wants to retire at age 62 and is 48 months from FRA. The worker's primary insurance amount is $2,640 per month due to DRCs. The worker's FRA benefits sere $2,000 per month. Therefore the 50 percent spousal benefit is $2,000 X 50% = $1,000 at FRA.

❖ Jane wants to receive benefits 48 months before FRA.
  o The reduction amount is 36 X 25/36 of one percent = 25 percent.
  o The reduction amount is 12 X 5/12 of one percent = 5 percent.

❖ The reduced spousal payment is $1,000 X 30 percent =$300.

❖ The monthly benefit amount is $1,000 - $300 = $700.

Table 2.2 How Early Retirement Reduces Claimant and Spousal Benefits

Full Retirement and Age 62 Benefit By Year Of Birth						
			At Age 62 (#3)			
Year of Birth (#1)	Full (Normal) Retirement Age	Months between Age 62 and Full Retirement Age (#2)	A $1,000 retirement benefit would be reduced to	The Retirement Benefit is Reduced by (#4)	A $500 spouse's benefit would be reduced to	The spouse's benefit is reduced by (#5)
1937 or earlier	65	36	$800	20.00%	$375	25.00%
1938	65 and 2 months	38	$791	20.83%	$370	25.83%
1939	65 and 4 months	40	$783	21.67%	$366	26.67%
1940	65 and 6 months	42	$775	22.50%	$362	27.50%
1941	65 and 8 months	44	$766	23.33%	$358	28.33%
1942	65 and 10 months	46	$758	24.17%	$354	29.17%
1943-1954	66	48	$750	25.00%	$350	30.00%
1955	66 and 2 months	50	$741	25.83%	$345	30.83%
1956	66 and 4 months	52	$733	26.67%	$341	31.67%
1957	66 and 6 months	54	$725	27.50%	$337	32.50%
1958	66 and 8 months	56	$716	28.33%	$333	33.33%
1959	66 and 10 months	58	$708	29.17%	$329	34.17%
1960 and later	67	60	$700	30.00%	$325	35.00%

1. If you were born on January 1st, you should refer to the previous year.

2. If you were born on the 1st of the month, we figure your benefit (and your full retirement age) as if your birthday was in the previous month. If you were born on January 1st, we figure your benefit (and your full retirement age) as if your birthday was in December of the previous year

3. You must be at least 62 for the entire month to receive benefits.

4. Percentages are approximate due to rounding.

5. The maximum benefit for the spouse is 50% of the benefit the worker would receive at full retirement age. The % reduction for the spouse should be applied after the automatic 50% reduction. Percentages are approximate due to rounding.

SOURCE: Social Security Administration (www.ssa.gov), 2012.

Table 2.2 shows that the percentage of reduction remains throughout the recipient's lifetime. For example, if reduction in spousal benefits is 30 percent when the recipient is 62 years old, it will still be a reduction of 30 percent when the recipient is at FRA and older. *Additionally, this rate of reduction continues even if the spouse later claims Social Security benefits based on his or her work record.*

Calculating Payment Amounts for Spouses with an Age Differences

The example in Table 2.3 is for a FRA benefit of $2,000 for a worker called Jake. FRA for Jake and his spouse Jane is age 66. Jane wants to retire 62 (she will be FRA in 48 months). Table 2.3 shows how much Jane will receive in spousal benefits if Jake retires at 62, 66 or 70 compared to Jane at age 62, 66 and 70.

If Jake takes early retirement and Jane takes early retirement, their joint monthly payment will be $2,025. In contrast, if Jake works until 70 and accrues DRCs he can increase his FRA benefit by 32 percent ($2, 640). If Jane waits until FRA she can collect 50 percent of Jake's FRA benefit ($1,000). By delaying retirement Jake and Jane will receive a monthly check of $3,640.

Table 2.3 Comparing Spousal Retirement Options

Monthly Benefit Amounts Differ Based on the Age of the Retired Worker			Spousal Benefits Vary Due to When the Worker Filed and Spouse's Age			
Earner's Age	Earner's Percentage Reduction	Monthly Benefit	Spouse's Age	50% Spousal Benefit	Percentage Reduction	Actual Monthly Benefit
62	75%	$1,500	62	$750	30%	$525
			66	$750	0%	$750
			70	$750	0%	$750
			First Survivor Benefit			$1,500
66	100%	$2,000	62	$1,000	30%	$700
			66	$1,000	0%	$1,000
			70	$1,000	0%	$1,000
			First Survivor Benefit			$2,000
70	132%	$2,640	62	$1,000	30%	$700
			66	$1,000	0%	$1,000
			70	$1,000	0%	$1,000
			First Survivor Benefit			$2,640

Note: The example in Table 2.3 is for a FRA benefit of $2,000 for a worker. FRA for the worker and the spouse is age 66. (Does not include COLAs.)

However, Table 2.3 is not the end of the discussion. When at least one spouse reaches FRA there are two maximizing strategies that become available the "Restricted Application" technique and the "File and Suspend" method.

❖ The Restricted Application approach is thoroughly explored in Chapter 5: Maximizing Your Benefits Now and Claiming More Later. In this chapter you'll uncover how the lower earner can claim benefits. Then the higher earner can claim spousal claim benefits on the lower earner's work record. Since the higher earner is FRA he or she can continue to accrue DRC and retire at 70 (some call this the 62 / 70 split).

❖ The File and Suspend strategy is investigated in Chapter 6: The "File and Suspend" Approach to Maximizing Benefits. Let's say that the high earner is FRA, the low earner is not FRA. The high earner files for benefits then immediately suspends the application. This allows the low earner to can claim spousal benefits while the high earner continues to work and can accrue DRCs to increase the high earner's benefits.

Should You Claim Benefits Based on Your Own Record or Your Spouse's Record?

If you are seeking a "quick" way to get a general idea of what may be best for your individual situation you may want to consider this approach.

❖ Go to the SSA Web site located at www.ssa.gov/estimator.

1. The SSA Retirement Estimator gives an estimate based on your actual Social Security earnings record. (The SSA reminds users that these are just estimates.) The SSA can't provide your actual benefit amount until you apply for benefits. Actual and estimated benefit amounts may differ for the following reasons:
    a. Your earnings may increase or decrease in the future.
    b. After you start receiving benefits, they will be adjusted for Cost-Of-Living increases (COLAs).
    c. Your benefit amount may be affected by military service, railroad employment or pensions earned through work on which you did not pay Social Security taxes.

❖ Estimate your benefits showing little or no additional work.

❖ Create a *second* estimate showing your current SSA taxable earnings continuing to FRA or age 70.

❖ If your spousal benefit is below the benefits you would receive on your own work record continue to work.

CHAPTER 3: MAXIMIZING SURVIVOR BENEFITS

Increasing monthly payments by maximizing survivor benefits works best for:
- ❖ working individuals widowed before their own retirement.
- ❖ low, mid or high earner widow(er)s who are seeking a strategy to maximize survivor benefits.
- ❖ individuals who want to increase their family's survivor benefits.

If you don't think that Social Security Survivor benefits are important, think again. Social Security provides 90 percent or more of income for 47 percent of all elderly unmarried women who receive benefits. Of course there are some limits. As in Chapter 2: Increasing Your Benefits by Utilizing Spousal Benefits let's begin with SSA definitions. The definitions and eligibility requirements for survivors are very similar to the definitions and eligibility requirements for spouses, ex-spouses and dependent family members. The following is a summary of how the SSA defines widow(er) s and survivors both in traditional and non-traditional unions:

Traditional Unions and Eligibility for Survivor Benefits

- ❖ **Widow(er):** According to the Social Security Handbook you are considered a widow(er) of the insured worker for Social Security purposes if under applicable law, if at the time the insured worker dies, you and the insured worker were validly married; or you would have the status of widow(er) with respect to the distribution of intestate personal property.

- ❖ *Ex-Spouse:* A surviving divorced spouse could also be eligible for a widow/widower's benefit on a worker's record.

- ❖ *Invalid Marriage:* Widow(er) of an invalid marriage that resulted from either a prior marriage or its dissolution and the defect in the procedure followed in connection with your marriage.
  - o You entered into a ceremonial marriage with the insured worker that was invalid under the law provided that you married the insured worker in good faith, not knowing of any impediment to the marriage.

o You were living with the insured worker in the same household at the time of his or her death.

o For periods prior to January 1991, there is no other person who is or was entitled to monthly insurance benefits on the insured worker's earnings record and still has the status as a legal widow(er).

❖ **Survivor Child(ren)** are unmarried and the worker's legitimate child, natural child, legally adopted child or stepchild. The child must be under 18 years old, or under age 19 and a full-time student in elementary or high school, or age 18 or over and totally disabled (with a disability that began before age 22). The survivor child (ren) is entitled to 75 percent of the worker's payment amount (which may be reduced due to family maximum benefit (FMB) restrictions.)

❖ **Survivor Parent(s)** are relatively rare due to the difficulty of qualifying as a dependent parent. To qualify the individual must be the natural parent of the worker, or became the worker's stepparent or adopting parent before the worker became age 16. The parent(s) must be dependent upon the deceased worker for at least 50 percent of their income and are 62 or older. If one parent is a claimant he or she receives 82.5 percent of the worker's full payment amount. If two parents are claimants, they receive 75 percent of the worker's benefit each (which may be reduced due to FMB restrictions.)

Benefits for Widow(er) s with a Disability

Normally widow(er) benefits do not begin until age 60. However, there is an exception to this rule if the widow(er) was disabled prior to the death of the worker. The widow(er) must be between the ages of 50 and 60, the widow(er) must meet the SSA definition of disabled, and the disability must have started before the death of the worker or within seven years after the worker's death. It is important to note that a widow(er) cannot apply online for survivors benefits based on their disability. Individuals can get the process started by completing a Disability Assistance Report (downloadable at www.socialsecurity.gov/applyfordisability) and should contact the SSA for assistance.

Non-Traditional Unions and Eligibility for Survivor Benefits

The following is quoted from the Social Security Administration Web site (www.ssa.gov) and explains how individuals in what may be considered "non-traditional" relationships can qualify for survivor benefits. "Generally, a person can qualify for widow's or widower's benefits if he or she was married to the deceased worker for at least nine months before the worker died. *However, you do not need to be married to the worker for any specific length of time if (and I am quoting from the SSA Web site):*

❖ You are the mother or father of the worker's biological child;

❖ You legally adopted the worker's child while you were married to him or her and before the child attained age 18;

❖ You are the parent of a child who was legally adopted by the worker while you and the worker were married and before the child attained age 18;

❖ You and the worker were married and both of you legally adopted a child under age 18;

❖ You were entitled or potentially entitled to spouse's, widow(er)'s, parent's benefits or to childhood disability benefits on the record of a fully insured individual in the month before the month you married the deceased worker;

❖ You were entitled or potentially entitled to a widow(er)'s, child's (age 18 or over) or parent's insurance annuity under the Railroad Retirement Act (RRA) in the month before you married the deceased worker;

❖ The worker was married previously to an institutionalized spouse, but was not allowed to divorce him or her under state law. After the spouse died, he or she married you within 60 days;

❖ You were married to the worker at the time of his or her death, you had been married to and divorced from him or her before, and the previous marriage lasted nine months;

❖ The worker's death occurred in the line of duty while he or she was a member of a uniformed service serving on active duty;

❖ The worker's death was accidental. (Note: The worker's death is considered "accidental" only if he or she received bodily injuries through violent, external and accidental means and, as a direct result of the bodily injuries and independent of all other causes, died within three months after the day he or she received the injuries.)

Survivor Benefits for the "Unnatural" Death of the Worker

The SSA pays survivor benefits to spouses, children, and dependent parents of individuals who have committed suicide, been executed for a crime or died while perpetrating a crime. In other words, the SSA does not penalize survivors for the actions of the earner. Benefits are contingent upon meeting the usual SSA survivor guidelines. In the case of suicide, the spouse must have been married for at least nine-months to be eligible for widow(er)s benefits.

Family Maximum Benefit (FMB) Amounts

According to the Social Security Administration Handbook, each entitled member of the family of a worker will receive a monthly benefit. The total benefits for the family cannot exceed 150 to 180 percent of the worker's benefit amount.

The total benefits are divided among the entitled family members (as previously defined in this chapter). Keep in mind that the earner's benefit is never decreased. However, increasing the entitled dependents will divide the total benefits among this larger number, resulting in the lowering the benefit amount for each person. Next, as children get older and no longer receive survivor benefits, their share of the family benefit is returned to the FMB total and the remaining family members will receive an increase in benefits.

Today, many households include children from former marriages, stepchildren, adopted children and grandchildren. Often both parents work. And each parent has their own earning's record.

If each parent has a earning's record, the SSA uses a complex combination formula to determine the Combined Family Maximum limit. The SSA provides the following example of the distribution of survivor benefits due to the Combined Family Maximum limit.

Mr. and Mrs. Jones had eight children in the family group, five of whom were their natural children. The other three were Mr. Jones' stepchildren by a former marriage. Mr. Jones died and all the children and the widow became entitled on his earnings record. Mrs. Jones died shortly thereafter and her five natural children became entitled on her earnings record since it yielded the larger benefit for each (and had the higher benefit amount). Table 3.1 shows the distribution of benefits.

Table 3.1: Example of Adjusted Combination Family Maximum Limit

	Original	Adjusted
Ann Day	$151.00	$100.60
Bob Day	$151.00	$100.60
Sid Day	$151.00	$100.60
Total		$301.80
	Original	Adjusted
Mary Jones	$160.50	$124.60
Peter Jones	$160.50	$124.60
Charles Jones	$160.50	$124.60
Marvel Jones	$160.50	$124.60
Ruth Jones	$160.50	$124.60
Total		$623.00

SOURCE: Social Security Administration (www.ssa.gov), 2012.

Taxation, Working and Survivor Benefits

According to the SSA, you can work and receive survivor benefits at the same time. The taxation rules for retirement benefits and survivor benefits are generally the same. (For details see Chapter 2 the section titled, "Taxation of Social Security Retirement Benefits for Early Retirees".)

If you are younger than FRA and earn more than $14,640, your benefit amount will likely be reduced. The SSA will deduct $1 from your benefits for each $2 earned above $14,640. For individuals who reach FRA in 2012, the SSA will deduct $1 from benefits for each $3 earned above $38,880. In contrast, persons age 66 or older may keep all of their benefits no matter how much they earn. The SSA provides the following example:

Let's say that you file for Social Security benefits at age 62 in January 2012 and your payment will be $600 per month ($7,200 for the year). During 2012, you plan to work and earn $20,800 ($6,160 above the $14,640 limit). The SSA will withhold $3,080 of your Social Security benefits ($1 for every $2 you earn over the limit).

To do this, the SSA will withhold <u>all benefit payments from January 2012 to June 2012.</u> Beginning in July 2012, you would receive your $600 benefit and this amount would be paid to you each month for the *remainder of the year. In 2013, the SSA will pay you the additional $520 they withheld in June 2012.*

Defining Survivor Fully Insured and Currently Insured Benefits

Survivor benefits are based on the worker's record. To be eligible for retirement credits a worker must have 40 work credits. However, as discussed in the Introduction and Chapter 1: Increasing Your Benefits by Selecting the "Right" Application Date, if an individual dies before FRA his or her survivors are eligible for survivor benefits based on the amount of work credits the deceased earner has accrued. There are two ways to meet the survivor benefit requirement for work credits. That is to have *fully insured status* or *currently insured status.*

Fully insured status covers family members that are the most dependent on the worker for financial support. Fully insured benefits may be paid to your:

- ❖ Spouse
- ❖ Ex-spouse
- ❖ Dependent child or children
- ❖ Dependent parents

The second type of survivor insurance eligibility is "currently insured". To be currently insured the worker must have acquired at least six work credits in the 13-quarter period ending with the quarter in which they passed away. Eligible family members for survivor benefits for currently insured workers at the time of death include:

- ❖ Spouse
- ❖ Ex-spouse (only if caring for a dependent child or children)
- ❖ Dependent child or children

Table 3.2 indicates that the older the worker is the more work credits are needed to be "fully insured". It is important to note that 40 is the maximum number of work credits needed to be fully insured. Many individuals who are in their 30's or 40's have already accrued 40 work credits. Individuals who die before FRA and do not have 40 work credits can also be fully insured. For example, Table 3.2 shows that someone passing away at age 48 needs only 26 work credits to be fully insured.

Table 3.2 Work Credits Needed for Fully Insured Survivor Benefits

Work Credits Needed for Fully Insured Status		
Death at Age	Years of Work	Credits Needed
31 to 42	5	20
44	5 1/2	22
46	6	24
48	6 1/2	26
50	7	28
52	7 1/2	30
54	8	32
56	8 1/2	34
58	9	36
60	9 1/2	38
62 or older	10	40

Source: Social Secruity Administration (www.ssa.gov), 2012.

Survivor Eligibility Requirements and Benefit Amounts

The following survivors can claim a percentage of the worker's benefits. Additionally, a special one-time lump sum payment of $255 may be made to the spouse or minor children. For more information, refer to the SSA Web site for a publication titled, "Survivors Benefits" downloadable in PDF format at www.ssa.gov/pubs/10084.pdf .

The following is a summary of the eligibility requirements to receive survivor benefits and the pre-determined amounts that survivors can expect to receive.

Widow(er)
❖ FRA or older can receive 100 percent of the worker's full payment amount
❖ Age 60 can receive 71.5 percent of the worker's full payment amount
❖ Any age, while caring for the worker's entitled child can receive 75 percent the worker's full payment amount

Requirements:
● Must be currently unmarried, or
● Remarried after age 60

Surviving Divorced Spouse
- ❖ FRA or older can receive 100 percent of the worker's full payment amount
- ❖ Age 60 can receive 71.5 percent of the worker's full payment amount
- ❖ Any age, while caring for the worker's entitled child (child under 16 or disabled) can receive 75 percent the worker's full payment amount

Requirements:
- Married for at least 10 years or more
- Currently unmarried, or remarried after age 60
- Have child in care

The following are a few additional notes on eligibility and survivor benefit amounts:
1. Generally, the survivor benefit amount that family members can receive each month is about 150 to 180 percent of the worker's basic benefit rate.
2. Fully disabled widow(er) s or fully disabled surviving divorced spouses are eligible at ages 50 to 59 for survivor benefits.
3. Only five individuals can claim spousal (or ex-spousal) survivor benefits on one worker's record.

Claiming Options for Survivor Benefits

According to the SAA no one needs to work more than 10 years to qualify for any Social Security benefit. Additionally, as shown in Table 3.2 the younger you are the fewer years you need to work for your family to fully qualify for survivor benefits. For example, under a special rule, if you or your spouse has worked for only one and a half years in a three-year period just before death, benefits can be paid to your children and your spouse who is caring for the children. The SSA is quick to point out that the value of the survivor's insurance you have under Social Security is probably has more value of your individual life insurance.

Shuart, Weaver and Whitman (Financial Planning Association Web site, www.fpanet.org, April 25, 2012) state that the SSA allows widows to claim survivor's or widow(er)s benefits or claim benefits on their own work records. These claiming options, as discussed earlier, are called "Dual Entitlement". Dual entitlement allows widow(er) s and survivors to implement a claiming strategy that maximizes benefits. For example, a low earner widow(er) or survivor that is 62 can claim benefits on their own work record. At FRA the widow(er) or survivor can switch to the high earner widow(er) or survivor benefit and claim 100 percent of the deceased worker's benefit. This allows widow(er)s to avoid being permanently saddled with a reduced benefit.

The rules for widow(er)s benefits are somewhat different than the rules for family benefits. In my opinion, the SSA has fine-tuned the rules to provide widow(er)s with a great safety net. The following are a few examples:

❖ If the earner did not claim benefits and did not live to FRA his or her benefits are set at the amount he or she would have earned if he or she had lived to FRA.

❖ Widow(ers)s have "dual entitlement". In other words, they can claim either their Widow's Insurance Benefits or benefits based on their own work records.

❖ The widow(er)'s insurance benefits is 100 percent of the deceased worker's benefit plus DRCs amounts, if any.

❖ If the deceased worker retired early, the widow(er) will receive that payment or 82.5 percent of the FRA benefits whichever is greater.

Analyzing Widow (er) s and Surviving Ex-Spouse Claiming Options

The following shows a survivor benefit maximizing strategy example that illustrates how developing a claiming strategy can help boost survivor benefits. (There are three choices which make decision-making complex. Table 3.3 graphically compares the options and targets the best choice.)

Diana's FRA is 66 with a benefit of $800 based on her earning's record. Diana is currently 62 and eligible for a benefit of $600. At FRA Diana is eligible for a full survivor's benefit of $1,500 based on her deceased husband's earning's record. At age 62 she is eligible for a reduced survivor's benefit of $1,200 (a reduction of 48 months X .396 = 19% rounded). If Diana works until 70 she will receive DRCs increasing her monthly payment on her own work record to $1,056 ($800 X 1.32 = $1,056.) Diana has three alternatives:

1. At age 62 claim early retirement of **$600** on her own earning's record. Next at FRA switch to claim FRA survivor benefits of **$1,500** (plus COLAs for the rest of her life).

2. At age 62 claim reduced survivor benefits of **$1,200** (plus COLAs) for the rest of her life.

3. At age 62 claim reduced survivor benefits of $1,200 (plus COLAs) then work until 70. At 70 switch to her own benefits of **$1,056** per year.

Table 3.3 shows a comparison of Diana's options. The best choice is use the dual entitlement option that allows Diana to claim her reduced benefits ($600) on her own work record until FRA. At FRA Diana can claim the full-survivor benefit of $1,500. The difficulty of this approach is bridging the financial gap to FRA. The following is a brief summary of Diana's three options illustrated in Table 3.3:

❖ The claim own now, claim survivor benefits later option is the first line on the chart. This approach has the best outcome when at age 85 it is compared to the two other options.
❖ The claim reduced survivor benefits forever is the second line on the chart. This strategy starts off well but by age 85 can't keep up with the first selection of claim own now, claim survivor benefits later.
❖ The third line is the claim reduced survivor benefits now, claim own benefits later opportunity. This approach had the worst outcome of the three options.

Table 3.3 Comparison of Survivor Retirement Options

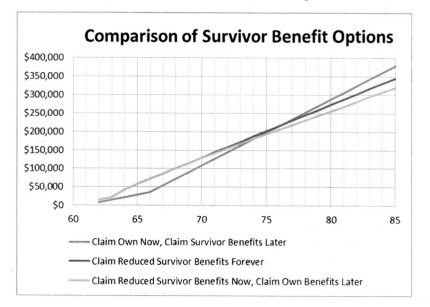

Survivor Benefits if the Deceased Worker Never Filed for Benefits

Widow(er) s and survivors can receive survivor benefits if the deceased worker has never filed for Social Security benefits. The following are is an example that illustrates what a widow(er) could expect to receive if he/she files at different ages.

Joyce has a FRA benefit of $1,000 based on her own work record. Joyce decides to retire at 62. Her benefit is reduced by 25 percent to $750. Joyce's husband's FRA benefit is $2,000. Joyce's husband dies before FRA and never claims retirement benefits. Joyce waits until she is FRA and claims widow benefits (100 percent of her husband's FRA retirement benefit). Joyce now receives a monthly widow's benefit of $2,000.

Survivor Benefits if the Deceased Worker has Delayed Retirement Credits

If the worker spouse dies, the surviving spouse can receive the same benefit as the worker spouse. If this benefit includes DRCs the surviving spouse can now receive DRCs benefits. The following is an example of how this works:

The FRA benefit for Dan was $1,000 per month. Dan worked to 70 and retired. Dan's monthly benefit increased by 32 percent (due to DRCs) to $1,320. At FRA Margaret claimed spousal benefits. When Margaret filed for FRA spousal benefits she received $500 per month (50 percent of Dan's FRA benefit). At age 71 Dan died and Margaret received survivor benefits equal to Dan's benefit of $1,320 per month. (And Margaret no longer receives her former spousal benefit.)

Calculating Survivor Benefits for a Deceased FRA Worker

Widow(er) s and survivors can receive less than 100 percent of the deceased worker's benefits for several reasons. First on the list is the early retirement of the widow(er) or survivor. According to the SSA, in 2005 about 30 percent of widow(er) benefits were paid to widow(er)s at or under their FRA. The following are a few items to keep in mind when you are developing a survivor claiming strategy: Widow(er) and survivor benefits can begin at any time between age 60 and FRA. Table 3.4 shows examples of age 62 survivor benefits based on a monthly FRA benefit of $1,000. (To determine how much your benefit will be reduced find the year of your birth.)

Table 3.4 Reduction of Survivor Benefits for Early Retirement

Year of Birth (a)	Full (Survivors) Retirement Age (b)	At age 62 (c) a $1,000 survivors benefits would be	Months between age 60 and full retirement age	Monthly % Reduction (d)
1939 or earlier	65		60	0.475
1940	65 and 2 months	$825	62	0.46
1941	65 and 4 months	$822	64	0.445
1942	65 and 6 months	$819	66	0.432
1943	65 and 8 months	$816	68	0.419
1944	65 and 10 months	$813	70	0.407
1945-1956	66	$810	72	0.396
1957	66 and 2 months	$807	74	0.385
1958	66 and 4 months	$805	76	0.375
1959	66 and 6 months	$803	78	0.365
1960	66 and 8 months	$801	80	0.356
1961	66 and 10 months	$798	82	0.348
1962 and later	67	$796	84	0.339

a. If you were born on January 1ₛ of any year, you should refer to the previous year.

b. If you were born on the 1st of the month, we figure your benefit (and your full retirement age) as if your birthday was in the previous month.

c. The $1000 benefit would be reduced to $715 for anyone who started receiving survivors benefits at age 60.

d. Monthly reduction percentages are approximate due to rounding. Your maximum benefit is limited to what your spouse would receive if he or she were still alive. Survivors benefits that start at age 60 are always reduced by 28.50%.

SOURCE: Social Security Administration (www.ssa.gov), 2012.

Using Table 3.4 the following shows how to determine survivor benefits at 60, 62, and FRA.

❖ **Retire at 60:** According to Table 3.4 if FRA is 66 and the widow(er) or survivor retires at 60, the benefits are permanently reduced to 71.5 percent of the total he or she would have received at FRA. In other words, in our example the survivor would receive $715.)

❖ **Retire at 62:** According to Table 3.4 if FRA is 66 and the widow(er) or survivor retires at 62 the benefit would be permanently reduced to 80.1% of the total he or she would have received at FRA. Here is the math so you can follow the calculation. First retirement is 48 months early. Thus 48 months X 0.396 = 19.008 percent). Therefore 100% -

19.008% = 80.992%. And $1,000 X .80992 = $810 (rounded). The monthly payment at age 62 is $810.

❖ **Retire at FRA:** There are no reductions in benefits when benefits are claimed at the FRA. If you take benefits before FRA, your benefits are reduced a fraction of a percent for each month before FRA. Table 3.2 shows the full retirement ages of survivors based on year of birth. Table 3.4 shows examples based on year of birth, age 62 survivors benefits based on a monthly benefit of $1,000 at FRA.

All Social Security benefits are based on two things. First, your full retirement age (FRA) which is currently 66. Second, the work record of the claimant. Let's say that you and your spouse are claiming social security benefits. For a married couple, the first survivor can claim the highest of the benefits but cannot claim both benefits (In other words, you can't claim survivor benefits and your own retirement benefits). Table 3.4 shows the reduction of survivor benefits for early retirement. The following narratives are several scenarios that examine how this affects different financial situations for widow(er)s.

Scenario #1 (Worker Filed at FRA, Spouse Files at age 60):
Your higher earning spouse receives a benefit of $1,000 per month. You are 60 years old and your higher earner spouse passes away. You apply for survivor Social Security benefits. However, you benefit is reduced for the rest of your life (See Table 3.4 for details). For example, if your FRA is 66 your survivor benefit is reduced by 28.5 percent if you claim at 60 years old. The survivor benefit is $715 per month for the rest of your life.

Scenario #2 (Worker Files at FRA, Spouse Files at age 62, then Files Survivor Benefits at FRA):
Let's say your spouse is the higher earner and has a FRA benefit of $1,000 per month. You claim benefits at age 62 on your own work record. Your benefits are reduced by 25 percent (from FRA $467 to $350). If you are now FRA and your higher earner spouse dies first, your benefit would be 100 percent of what your spouse received. If you apply at FRA for widow(er) benefits you will receive 100 percent of what your higher earner spouse's received. That is a $1,000 per month benefit and your current benefit of $350 will terminate.

Scenario #3 (Worker Filed at FRA, Spouse Files Early):
You are FRA and you are the higher earner spouse. Your receive
$1,000 per month. Your FRA lower earner spouse, who is collecting
spousal benefits of $500 per month, passes away. As the higher earner
spouse you continue to receive your monthly benefit of $1,000. The
smaller benefit of $500 is terminated.

Determining Survivor Benefits for Deceased Non-FRA Worker

If the worker spouse dies before filing for benefits, survivors can still claim benefits. *In this situation, the amount paid is based on the anticipated FRA benefit at the time of death.* Additionally, children and dependent parents of the deceased worker can receive benefits (up to the family maximum which is generally 150 to 180 percent of the deceased worker's benefit. (See more about surviving children and parent benefits at the end of this chapter.)

Table 3.5 is a summary of the widow (er) benefits at different ages for a deceased spouse age 64 who passes away at age without filing for benefits.

Table 3.5 Survivor Benefits for Deceased Worker who has Never Filed

Spouse Never Filed for Social Security, FRA 66 Benefit $2,000 Per Month Widow(er) FRA 66 Applies for Survivor Benefits			
Spouses Age at Death 64, Benefit $2,000	Survivor Begins Benefits at:	Age	Survivor Benefit
		60	$1,430
		62	$1,620
		64	$1,810
		66	$2,000

❖ The expected FRA benefit for the deceased worker is $2,000. If the survivor (with a FRA of 66) applies for benefits at age 60 he or she will receive $1,430. This is 71.5 percent of the $2,000 benefit ($2,000 X .715 = $1,430).

❖ Table 3.5 goes on to indicate that if the survivor applies for benefits at age 62 the benefit will be reduced to $1,620. Refer to Table 3.2 for the amount of reduction per month then multiply this factor (.0396) by the number of months from full retirement (48) for 48 X .0396 = 19.01 percent. Therefore 100 percent − 19.01 percent = 81 percent (rounded). If the survivor applies at age 62 for benefits, the following formula is used $2,000 X .81 = $1,620.

❖ If the survivor retires at age 64 that's 24 months before retirement. Using Table 3.2 to determine the reduction per month (0.396) and multiplying it times the number of months from full retirement (24). Therefore 24 X .0396 = 9.5 percent. Therefore 100 percent − 9.5 percent = 90.5 percent. If the survivor applies at age 64 for benefits, the following formula is used $2,000 X .905 = $1,810.

❖ Table 3.5 concludes by showing how the survivor will receive 100 percent ($2,000) of the survivor benefit if he or she waits until FRA to apply for survivor benefits.

Assessing Survivor Benefits for Deceased Early Retiree

If your spouse (or ex-spouse) started to receive retirement benefits before FRA, the SSA determines the maximum survivors can receive based on the anticipated FRA amount if the worker was still alive. In other words, the earnings record and the anticipated earnings of the worker spouse may not be the same. For information about how to calculate the exact amount of your widow(er)s or survivor benefit refer to the SSA Web site located at secure.ssa.gov/apps10/poms.nsf/lnx/0200204045!opendocument#e   or contact your SSA representative to get an estimate at 1-800-772-1213 (TTY 1-800-325-0778) 7 a.m. to 7 p.m., Monday through Friday.

The Earlier Survivors Claim the Less They Receive

Let's assume that your spouse, due to ill health or for some other reason, files early for retirement benefits. *This limits survivors to that same reduced payment or an 82.5 percent payment reduction of the FRA benefit whichever is greater.* Additionally, the earlier survivors claim benefits the less they will receive.

Standard Survivor Benefit Claiming Examples

The following are two examples that illustrate two strategies for claiming survivor benefits. One strategy is for a FRA survivor and the other strategy is for an early retirement survivor.

Scenario #1 (Early worker retirement, FRA survivor retirement): Fran's husband died when Fran was FRA at 66. Her husband, Scott (an *early retiree) had a FRA of 66 and FRA benefit of $2,000. Fran has several options, she can claim the same reduced payment that he late husband received or she can claim an 82.5 percent of her husband's FRA benefit. Due to Scott's retirement at age 62 he received a monthly benefit of $1,500. When Scott died Fran had two options: (1) Claim 100 percent of Scott's monthly benefit ($1,500) or (2) Claim 82.5 percent of Scott's FRA benefit of $2,000 ($1,650). Therefore Fran will receive the larger benefit of $1,650. (Keep in mind that FRA Fran can collect survivor's benefits and continue to work.)*

Scenario #2 (Early worker retirement, early survivor retirement): John was 62 years old when he began to draw benefits. His FRA benefit was $2,000 but due to early retirement at 62 John received $1,500. At 63 years old John dies and his wife Irene, age 60, immediately starts widow benefits ($2,000 X .715) for $1,430 (rounded) per month. If Irene had waited until her FRA she would have received $1,650 per month ($2,000 X .82.5 = $1,650).

Optimization Strategies for Widows(er) s and Survivors

Statistics indicate that most spouses live for at least ten-years after the death of their spouse. Increased survivor benefits can make those years for the surviving spouse more comfortable. Social Security provides 90 percent or more of income for 47 percent of all elderly unmarried women who receive benefits. This statistic shows the importance of selecting a survivor claiming strategy that makes the most of your Social Security benefits. Shuart, Weaver and Whitman in their article for the Financial Planning Association Web site (www.fpanet.org, April 2012) provide analyses of the **optimal claiming strategies** for widow(er) s and divorced survivors. The author's suggest that most the most favorable strategies may be as follows:

Scenario #1 (Survivors with no or low earnings records):
Widow(er) s or survivors with no earnings or low earnings (that is around 20 percent of the deceased workers FRA benefit) should claim widow's benefits at 60. Often these widow(er) s or survivors do not have the financial resources to wait until FRA. However, if they can bridge the financial gap until FRA they will receive a higher monthly benefit. A higher monthly payment is a good way to cover longevity risk. For example, if the deceased worker's benefit is $1,000 per month, the widow(er) or survivor will permanently receive $715 per month if he or

she claims at 60 years old. If the widow(er) or survivor can wait until FRA the benefit will be $1,000 per month.

Scenario #2 (Survivors with moderate earnings records):

Widow(er) s or survivors with moderate earning records (around 50 percent of the benefit for the deceased worker) should take their own retirement benefits at age 62. At the widow(er) or survivor's FRA he or she should take the widows insurance benefit which is 100 percent of the deceased worker's benefit. If the worker's benefit is $1,000 per month, the widow(er) or survivor will permanently receive $810 per month.

Scenario #3 (Survivors with high earnings records):

Widow(er) s or survivors with high earning records should take the widows insurance benefit early, then at 70 years old switch to their own earnings record and claim benefits. For example, at 60 years-old the claim would be $715 if the deceased worker's FRA benefit is $1,000 per month. The widow(er) or survivor should work until 70 years old.

Let's say that using his or her own work record, the FRA benefit for the Widow(er) or survivor is $1,500. With four years of delayed retirement credits (DRCs) the FRA amount increases by 32 percent ($1,500 X .32 = $480). The high earner widow(er) or survivor's new monthly payment amount on his or her own record is $1,980.

CHAPTER 4: GETTING MORE BY RETRACTING YOUR APPLICATION AND REFILING (THE "RESET)

The Reset Strategy works best for:

- ❖ individuals or married couples who change their minds about claiming Social Security Benefits within a one-year time period.
- ❖ individuals or married couples who don't want to touch their savings while they are temporarily out of work.

Instructions for the "Reset" Approach

During the first 12-months that you begin to receive your Social Security benefit you may want to withdraw your application (you have changed your mind about when you want to start drawing Social Security benefits). During this 12-month period, you can withdraw your application and re-apply for SSA at a future date.

This is a once in a lifetime SSA approved option.

Some individuals use the "Reset" methodology to "borrow" funds for up to 12-months. This method may be effective for someone who has savings that can't be touched without incurring a large penalty and needs cash now. In other words, the "Reset Methodology" is one way to solve an immediate cash flow problem and still get higher benefit payments later in life.

However, "resetting" does have its risks. Once your Withdrawal Application is approved by the SSA, which is almost automatic, you must repay all benefits that you have already received as per your original retirement application.

A benefit of this approach is that it is similar to buying an immediate annuity, except that you don't have to pay any interest on the benefits you've already received and there are no fees. Additionally, if you repay benefits in the same year your receive Social Security benefits, there are no tax ramifications. The biggest hurdle for this strategy is that you must have the *repayment* money on-hand when you need it.

To repay the benefits you received write a check to the U.S. Treasury and a short letter stating why you are returning the benefit. You can send your check and letter via U.S. Postage Service Return Receipt to the Regional Financial Center (RFC), U.S. Treasury Department. If you prefer you can return the benefit amount to your local Social Security office. Your Social Security office will give you a receipt for the check and will forward the check to the U.S. Treasury Department.

In the past, the Reset Strategy was popular because it was similar to a "no interest loan" that allowed folks to restart benefits at a later date to take advantage of a higher payout. Due to the lack of restraints individuals could reset as many times as they wanted. When the SSA became aware of the "no interest loan" aspect of this approach they limited resetting.

In 2008 a Social Security Administration report stated that in 2007 about 26,000 Social Security claimants "Reset" their applications. After much public discussion, as of December 8, 2010, the SSA announced that this option would henceforth be limited to one year's worth of benefits, once in a lifetime. Changing this provision made an immediate difference to the number of withdrawal applications. According to Mark Lassiter (2010) the SSA in fiscal 2009 reported that around 1,015 withdrawal applications were processed and in the first half of 2010 about 345 claimants reset their applications.

For example, let's say you elected to receive early benefits at age 62. You're now approaching your 63rd birthday and thinking of going back to work. You could stop receiving retirement benefits, pay back the one year's worth of benefits you received, go back to work, and then wait until a later age to restart your benefit at a higher level.

At that later date when SSA recalculates your higher benefit, your spouse and survivors will also receive benefits based on your stepped-up level.

To take advantage of the "Reset" approach you will need to use a one-page request form titled, Withdrawal Application Form SSA-521. This SSA-521 form is downloadable in PDF format from the SSA Web site at www.ssa.gov/online/ssa521.pdf.

You may be wondering about the tax implications of your repayment to the SSA. For more information about the tax consequences of the Reset Strategy, the SSA provides an online publication titled, "If You Change Your Mind" located at www.ssa.gov/retire2/withdrawl.htm.

The Reset Approach: Use With Caution

Deciding if the Reset Strategy makes sense for you depends on many factors such as, your tax situation, age and life expectancy. Keep in mind that you can't reverse the "Reset" strategy. For example, the week following your repayment to Social Security, if you are accidentally killed your family cannot reclaim the lump sum you just paid back.

CHAPTER 5: "CLAIM NOW AND CLAIM MORE LATER" TO BOOST MONTHLY BENEFITS

The Claim Now and Claim More Later Strategy (also called the "Restricted Application Strategy") works best for:
- married working couples where each has a Social Security earnings record.
- the higher earner who works past his/her FRA.
- FRA high earners who want to claim "free spousal benefits" on the low earner's record while working

For Marrieds Only: The Restricted Application Approach

Please note that this is a **married only** strategy because it uses spousal benefits while the higher earner accrues delayed retirement credits (DRCs). (the term "Married" is defined in Chapter 2: Increasing Your Benefits by Utilizing Spousal Benefits.) The technique is also called the "Restricted Application" approach. The restricted application method is used when the lower earner spouse retires early, retires at FRA or retires after FRA.

Ideally, at FRA the higher earner spouse claims spousal benefits on the lower earner's work record using a "restricted application". *Keep in mind, the higher earner spouse is not claiming his or her own retirement benefits.* In other words the higher earner wants to "restrict" the retirement application to spousal benefits only.

CAUTION: You cannot file a restricted application online.

Next, the high earner continues to work and claims his or her own increased benefits between the ages 66 and 70. Currently, if the higher earner continues to work up to age 70, he (or she) will increase FRA benefits by 32 percent (that's eight percent per year).

The high earner's spouse can now claim spousal benefits on the high earner's work record (if it results in a monthly benefit that is greater than the low earner's current benefit).

The Restricted Application approach allows the married couple to optimize their lifetime monthly benefit amount. An additional advantage of this approach (and to my way of thinking the most important aspect of this approach) is the increase to the survivor benefit.

The Center for Retirement Research at Boston College (August 2009) states that the main beneficiaries of Restricted Application strategy tend to be two-earner couples, with higher than average salaries, and estimates that the "Claim Now and Claim More Later Strategy" has an annual cost to the SSA of about $9.7 billion. Specifically, the "claim now and claim more later" approach is a good claiming strategy for working married couples, where the higher earner is full retirement age (FRA), and if both are FRA and one or both continue to work after retirement benefits begin.

The File and Suspend Strategy Versus the Restricted Application Strategy

The restricted application policy discussed in the Chapter 5: Maximizing Your Benefits by Claiming Now and Claiming More Later is when the high earner collects spousal benefits. In contrast, Chapter 6: The "File and Suspend" Approach to Maximizing Benefits investigates how the spouse of the high earner in the File and Suspend strategy collects benefits while the high earner continues accruing DRCs. For examples of comparisons of the cumulative payments for each methodology see Appendix A.

According to the SSA each application form is clearly worded to show its scope as an application for one or more types of benefits. You may apply for all benefits on any Social Security earnings record or you can *restrict* your application to a *"spouse only benefit"* by adding appropriate remarks in writing.

Ex-Spouses and the Restricted Application Strategy

Ex-spouses can use the restricted application strategy to increase their retirement nest eggs. For divorced women who plan to work until age 70 the Restricted Application Strategy is ideal for "catching up" on needed retirement funds. The FRA ex-spouse can apply for spousal benefits on the earner's work record and continue to work. The ex-spouse can gain DRCs until 70. At age 70 the ex-spouse can switch to her own larger benefit.

If there is any discussion about filing a Restricted Application, please refer to Social Security POMS GN 00204.040 Scope of Application Rule, Section D. Policy- Restricting the Scope of the Application which states,

"The claimant may choose to limit or restrict the scope of the application to exclude a class of benefits he/she may be eligible to on one or more SSNs for any reason (except when deemed filing applies). The reason may be to receive higher current benefits or to maximize the amount of benefits over a period of time, including the effect of delayed retirement credits (DRCs)."

A Comparison of the Traditional and Restricted Application Approaches

The following is a comparative example of how the "claim now and claim more later" strategy works. For this example, I am going to say that Joe is the higher earner.

Table 5.1 is a side-by-side comparison of the traditional approach and the restricted application strategy.

1. *Both Jane and Joe are FRA and 66 years old. If Jane retires now on her own work record she will receive $1,000 per month in benefits. Joe plans to work until he is 70 years old. If he retires now he will receive $1,500 per month in benefits. If he retires at age 70 he will receive benefits of 32 percent more per month (for a total of $1,980).*

2. *Using the claim now and claim later strategy. Jane will retire and claim her FRA benefit of $1,000 per month; Joe will claim spousal benefits of $500 per month on Jane's work record until he retires at age 70.*

3. *When Joe retires, Jane has the option of switching to claiming spousal benefits on Joe's work record. Jane's spousal benefits will be 50 percent of Joe's FRA benefit ($750) which is less than her current benefit. Therefore Jane will continue to claim her own benefits.*

The left column of Table 5.1 shows the cumulative payments for a married couple applying for their own benefits at FRA. Using the Traditional Approach at 66 Joe and Jane each claim their own benefits for a total of $2,500. The right column of Table 5.1 indicates the cumulative payments for the couple if they use the Restricted Application approach. At 66 Jane claims her own $1,000 a month benefit and Joe files a restricted application for spousal benefits only (on Jane's earning's record) and receives $500 per month. Joe works until 70 accruing DRCs and re-applies for benefits. (Joe's spousal benefits cease). At age 85 the yield of the Restricted Application Approach is greater than the Traditional Approach. See Table 5.2 for a graphical illustration of this comparison.

Table: 5.1 Comparisons of the Traditional Approach and the Restricted Application Strategy for a Married Couple at FRA

FRA Traditional Approach	FRA Restricted Application Plan
Jane claims 100% of her own $1,000 FRA benefit at age 66. Joe claims 100% of his own FRA $1,500 benefit at age 66.	Jane Claims 100% of Her Own at 66 ($1,000), Joe Draws a 50% Spousal Claim at 66, Joe's FRA benefit is $1,500, Joe Claims His Own at age 70 and Draws 132% ($1,980).
At 66, Jane files for payments of $1,000 per month (Claiming on her own record provides a bigger benefit than spousal benefits). At 66, Joe files for payments of $1,500 per month. (Total benefits are $2,500 per month)	At 66, Jane claims 100% of her own benefits of $1,000 per month At 66, Joe files a "restricted application" for spousal benefits only and claims a 50% spousal benefit of $500 per month on Jane's work record. Joe continues to work and accrues DRCs. (The couple receives $1,500 per month)
At 70, total cumulative payments = **$150,000**	At 70, total cumulative payments = **$107,760**
At 70 no further action	At 70 Joe files for benefits of $1,980 per month. This is 100% of FRA amount $1,500 plus 32% of FRA benefit for DRCs ($480). Jane continues with FRA benefits of $1,000 (The couple receives $2,980 per month)
At 85 total cumulative payments = **$600,000**	At 85 total cumulative payments = **$644,160**
At 95 total cumulative payments = **$900,000**	At 95 total cumulative payments = **$1,001,760**
First death survivor receives $1,500 per month	First death survivor receives $1,980 per month

Note: This example does not include Cost-Of-Living Adjustments (COLAs), Medicare deductions, or other adjustments.

To successfully implement the restricted application approach you must be a married couple, where at least one individual is FRA and working.

❖ Apply for your own retirement benefits, then immediately "restrict" your application. Otherwise when you continue working you will not accrue DRCs. (Keep a certified copy of your application to make certain that you have your "Restricted Application" in writing.)

❖ Apply for spousal benefits on your spouse's work record. (Keep in mind that, only one person receives spousal benefits at a time. That is, you both cannot receive spousal benefits at the same time.)

❖ Re-apply for your own benefits at age 70. Spousal benefits will cease.

❖ Currently, if you work until age 70 your monthly benefit will be 32 percent greater than your FRA benefit.

❖ Any Cost-Of-Living (COLAs) percentage increases will be based on your increased payment amount. The higher your benefit amount the greater the COLA benefit based on the percentage of increase.

❖ The high earner's monthly benefit is equal to the first death survivor benefit. Therefore if the high earner works four years after FRA he or she will increase the FRA benefit by 32 percent and increase the survivor benefit by 32 percent.

Table 5.2 Break-Even Age for the FRA Restricted Application Example

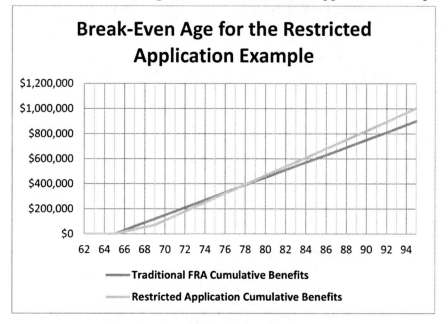

Table 5.2 indicates that 78 is the break-even age for the Restricted Application Approach example shown in Table 5.1. In other words, for this approach to be effective the couple should live to at least age 78. However, if Joe passes away before reaching 70 years old, the DRCs will be applied to Jane's benefit. For many individuals the increase in the survivor benefit is worth working after FRA.

Examples of Online Maximizing Calculators and Programs

Currently, there are several robust online Social Security maximization calculators and software programs that can assist you in determining the optimal claiming strategy for your personal financial circumstances. These Web sites may be good sources for ideas that can point you in the right direction. The fees charged for online calculators or software programs vary from free to several hundred dollars with live expert help. Samples of these online resources are listed below in alphabetical order:

Maximize My Social Security (www.maximizemysocialsecruity.com) is a powerful online calculator designed to show you the best time to apply for Social Security benefits for your individual financial situation. The cost is $40 for consumers and $200 for financial planners (who can use the online calculator for their clients). The comprehensive program requires you to enter your earnings record from your individual Social Security Statement (located at www.socialsecurity.gov/mystatement/) facts about your personal financial situation, and forecasts of expected earnings. The program will run calculations for optimal claiming strategies for singles, couples, survivors, ex-spouses, and adult and child dependents. Maximize My Social Security is one of the few programs that includes calculations for Government Offset Provisions (GOP) and Windfall Elimination Provisions (WEP). (For details about GOP and WEP see Chapter Eight: What Can Reduce Your Benefits.)

Social Security Strategy Analyzer (www.socialsecuritysolutions.com) provides three types of analyses: (1) Do-it-yourself for consumers. (2) Do it with expert advice for consumers and (3) a professional version of their software for financial advisers for $1,200.
* ❖ The "Do it yourself" consumer version has two options (1) purchasing a 16-page downloadable report for $19.45 with a recommended solution or (2) purchasing a deluxe "do-it-yourself" package for $49.95 with for a recommended solution and interactive tools. The interactive tools allow you to create and compare claiming strategies.
* ❖ Security Solutions financial specialists are also available. There are two financial adviser assisted consumer packages available. The first assisted package is a recommended solution and advice from an

expert for $124.95. The second package is $249.95 which includes the first expert assisted package, and then the financial adviser files your application and monitors your financial situation. (There are also hourly charges for personalized help.)

Social Security Income Planner (www.ssincomeplanner.com/servlet/init) is an online calculator that charges from $10 to $40 depending on your status (single, married, divorced, or survivor) per optimal strategy report. The calculator uses pre-selected age combinations and claiming strategies (strategies for couples include Restricted Application, File and Suspend, and strategies for singles include applying at the right time for wage earner, survivor and spousal or ex-spousal benefits.) You can also enter your own claiming strategy. Results are in tables that allow you to compare strategies and indicate the optimal strategy.

Social Security Timing (www.socialsecuritytiming.com) uses software that examines 81 possible age combinations across nine possible claiming strategies to find your optimal claiming strategy. Consumers seeking details on their free Social Security Timing reports have agreed to talk to an adviser and are prompted to contact a financial adviser listed in the Social Security Timing Directory for details. In addition to the free online report, Social Security Timing offers training modules, a downloadable brochure, and a free 10-day trial. Financial advisers are encouraged to subscribe for $21.99 per month. Financial advisory firms that subscribe get software tools to generate client reports. (Client reports have the ability to use the financial adviser's logo, the financial adviser's contact information, the firm's disclosures, and a micro Web site). Financial advisory firms are listed in a Social Security Timing Directory that includes contact information and a link to the financial adviser's Web site.

CHAPTER 6: THE FILE AND SUSPEND APPROACH TO MAXIMIZING BENEFITS (THE "62 / 70 SPLIT")

The File and Suspend Strategy (also called the "62 /70 Split) Approach works best for:

❖ FRA individuals who want to suspend retirement payments while accruing DRCs.

❖ married couples where the higher earner wants to accrue DRC while the spouse claims spousal benefits.

❖ married couples that want to combine the restricted application and file and suspend strategies.

File and Suspend, Another "Marrieds Only" Approach

When I contemplate the File and Suspend Strategy I think of it as "leveraging". That is, the File and Suspend Strategy is one way working couples can leverage their hard work to boost their monthly Social Security benefits. The file and suspend strategy works best for couples that have unequal salaries. In other words, the bigger the difference in the salaries the better the approach. If the salaries are about the same, then there is no advantage to filing and suspending. For example, if a 50 percent spousal benefit is less than the spouse's own retirement benefit, the spouse should file for his or her own benefit.

The File and Suspend strategy was enacted in 2000 as part of the "Senior Citizen's Freedom to Work Act". This Act also encourages individuals to work after FRA by eliminating the annual retirement earning test (See Chapter Seven: How Working after Retirement Can Increase Your Benefits for details).

Please keep in mind that there are various ways that a File and Suspend Strategy can be "fine-tuned" to fit individual financial situations. Overall, the strategy allows spouses to claim benefits while high earners accrue Delayed work Credits (DRCs) once he or she has reached FRA.

The File and Suspend Procedure Step-by-Step

The basic theory of the File and Suspend Strategy is that individuals who do not collect benefits today will accumulate higher benefits for later. Here are step-by-step instructions for the File and Suspend Strategy:

The strategy begins with the FRA higher-earning spouse (husband or wife) filing for Social Security benefits at FRA but immediately **filing a notice to suspend benefits.**

1. The non-working or lower-earning spouse (husband or wife) files for spousal benefits. Preferably, the lower earner spouse receives a spousal benefit that is greater than the benefit he or she would have received on his or her own work record.

    a. If the spouse filing for spousal benefits is FRA he or she will receive 50 percent of the earner's benefit.

    b. If the spouse filing for spousal benefits is younger than FRA he or she will receive a reduced spousal benefit

2. The higher-earning spouse continues to work and accrue DRCs. The DRCs of 8 percent per year increase the higher-earning spouse's monthly benefit.

3. If the earner dies before filing for benefits at age 70, the spouse will receive monthly benefits that include the DRCs.

4. One of the advantages of the File and Suspend methodology is a bigger survivor benefit and larger Cost-Of-Living (COLAs) amounts due to the increased amount of the monthly payment.

The Center for Retirement Research at Boston College (2009) estimates that the annual cost of the File and Suspend strategy to the SSA is around $1 billion per year. (Compared to the cost of over $9 billion per year for individuals using the Restricted Application methodology.) To be eligible for the File and Suspend Strategy you must be FRA but not yet 70 years old and want to accrue DRCs.

The SSA needs time to process your request. Social Security benefits are paid the month after they are due. Therefore if you contact the SSA in June and request suspension of your benefits, you may receive your June benefit payment in July. If this happens don't worry, just return the payment and verify that you have actually suspended payments. (Instructions about how to safely return funds to the SSA are detailed later in this chapter.) To sum it up, you can suspend current and future benefit payments up to age 70 and your spouse can claim spousal benefits while you accrue DRCs.

The File and Suspend Strategy if the Spouse is Not Yet FRA

There are a few wrinkles in the File and Suspend Approach if the lower-earning spouse is below FRA. First, the lower-earning spouse (husband or wife) must be at least 62 years old to claim spousal benefits. If the lower-earning spouse it below FRA then the SSA will investigate his or her work record. If the work record results in a monthly benefit that is greater than the monthly spousal benefit, then the spouse must claim his or her own benefits thus negating the File and Suspend Strategy. **In other words, they will be filing for their own benefits at age 62.**

In the Future Expect Benefit Reductions to Increase

As the age for claiming full Social Security benefits increases persons who retire at 62 will see a greater reduction in their Social Security Benefits. For example, Social Security benefits will be reduced by 30 percent for a person who retires at age 62 whose FRA is 67 (those born in 1960 or later). *(The Social Security Amendments of 1983, H.R. 1900 Public Law 98-21) increase the normal retirement age to 67.*

The Fine Print about the File and Suspend Approach

You can File and Suspend if you are FRA but not yet 70 years old. If you have filed for benefits and the SSA has not made a determination about your benefits, you can suspend benefits. Additionally, you can suspend benefits for any month for which you have not received a payment. In other words, you can suspend any retroactive benefits.

Get it in Writing

You can File and Suspend your benefits orally or in writing. It is the policy of the SSA that you do not have to sign your request to suspend benefit payments. However, I would err on the side of caution and get it in writing. At 70 years old you don't want to discover that you really didn't accrue DRCs.

If you are already entitled to benefits (up to age 70) and suspend beginning the month after the month when you first made your request you will likely receive a payment for one month's benefits. For example, if you suspend in January you will receive your January benefit in February via direct deposit to your checking account. When this happens write a check to the U.S. Treasury and a short letter stating why you are returning the benefit. You can send your check and letter via U.S. Postage Service Return Receipt to the Regional Financial Center (RFC), U.S. Treasury Department. If you prefer you can return the benefit amount to your local Social Security office. Your Social

Security office will give you a receipt for the check and will return the check to the U.S. Treasury Department.

A Potential "Gotcha" for Medicare and the File and Suspend Strategy

In July 2012 Laurence Kotlikoff, Professor of Economics Boston University and President of Economic Security Planning, Inc., in an article for *Making Sense* (www.pbs.org/newshour/fundown/2012/07/social-security-secrets-you-need-to-know-now.html) stated that if you select the File and Suspend approach and don't pay your Medicare Part B premiums via your own checking account the consequences can be severe. The SSA will pay your Medicare premium for you and deem you as waiving your suspension of benefits and you won't accrue DRCs. To sum it up, if you don't pay your Medicare Part B premiums from your own checking account, when you retire your benefit will be no greater than when it was on the day you suspended benefits. The monthly Medicare payment for 2012 is $99.90. For more information and exceptions to this rule see www.medicare.gov/default.aspx.

A Few Pointers Before Implementing the File and Suspend Strategy

A few items to keep in mind when using the File and Suspend strategy are:
- ❖ To File and Suspend you must be FRA.
- ❖ Either spouse can File and Suspend, but not both. In other words, by suspending both of you will not qualify for spousal benefits at the same time.
- ❖ *If the non-suspending spouse is below FRA he or she cannot receive DRCs on his or her record. Additionally, the percentage of reduction for early retirement will never go away*
- ❖ The File and Suspend strategy can be complex. Before putting it into practice, check with your financial adviser or CPA, and double-check with the SSA for any changes in the regulation.
- ❖ It is important to note that the FRA individual that files and suspends can always re-file on their own earning's record.
- ❖ At FRA and later, a non-suspending individual has the option of claiming his or her own benefits or the spousal benefit (but not both).
- ❖ For more information about the File and Suspend claiming strategy see www.ssa.gov/retire2/suspend.htm.

Ways to Get a Big Check: File for Back Payments

If you are six months older than full retirement age and have not yet filed for benefits, you can request benefits to start when you turned FRA. New claimants are allowed a "claw-back" of up to six months which allows them to receive "back pay".

For FRA individuals using the File and Suspend strategy, this approach is a way to get a big check. After filing and suspending you may set a start date that goes back to your application date. Depending on when you originally filed and suspended (and turned FRA) your start date can be anywhere from several months to several years. Filing your claim starts monthly payments and triggers back pay.

A Comparison of the Traditional and File and Suspend Strategy

The following in Table 6.1 is a practical example that illustrates step-by-step how the File and Suspend strategy works:

Table 6.1 provides a 62 / 70 Split example of the "File and Suspend" claiming approach for an early retiree and FRA claimant compared to the traditional approach.

1. *Janet (who works part-time in a local department store) will take early retirement at age 62. Janet's monthly FRA benefit is $700. If she retires at age 62 she will receive 75 percent ($525) of her FRA benefit.*
2. *Janet's husband James FRA is 66 and the FRA benefit is $2,000. James plans to File and Suspend his benefits at his FRA and work until 70. When James files and suspends, Janet will be able to claim spousal benefits.*
3. *At FRA Janet will claim spousal benefits on James work record. At this point Janet's benefits will change. Due to Janet's early retirement she will continue to receive $525 of her own benefit, plus spousal benefits for a total of $825 in monthly benefits. (For details see Chapter 2: Increasing Your Benefits by Utilizing Spousal Benefits.)*

4. *James will continue to work until he is 70. James benefit will grow at 8 percent per year. At age 70 James will re-apply for benefits and receive $2,640 per month.*

Table 6.1 Side-by-Side Comparisons of the Traditional Approach and the File and Suspend Strategy.

Traditional Approach At FRA James Draws 100% at 66, and Janet files for FRA Spousal Benefits for a total of $3,000	File and Suspend Approach Janet at 62 Claims of 75% of Her Own, James at FRA Files and Suspends, Janet at FRA Switches to Spousal Benefits, at 70 James re-applies and receives his FRA benefit and DRCs of 32%.
At 62 no action	At 62 Janet claims her own benefits of $525 until age 66 At 66 total payments = **$31,500**
At 66, James files for FRA payments of $2,000, and Janet files for FRA spousal benefits of $1,000. Total monthly payment $3,000.	At 66, James files and suspends. Janet claims spousal payments for a total of $825 per month.
At 70, total payments = **$180,000**	At 70, total payments = **$71,100**
James at 70 no action.	At 70 John files for benefits of $2,640 per month (32% increase of FRA amount due to DRCs). Janet continues to receive $825 per month. Total monthly payment $3,465.
At 85 total payments = **$720,000**	At 85 total payments = **$694,800**
At 95 total payments = **$1,008,000**	At 95 total payments = **$1,110,600**
First death survivor receives $2,000 per month.	First death survivor receives $2,640 per month.

Note: This example does not include Cost-Of-Living Adjustments (COLAs), Medicare deductions, or other adjustments.

Table 6.1 shows how the Traditional approach compares to the File and Suspend strategy. In this example James and Janet are the same age. The Traditional approach has no action until FRA. At FRA James claims his FRA benefit of $2,000 per month and Janet claims her FRA spousal benefit of

$1,000. The couple receives $3,000 per month. At 70 the Traditional approach has cumulative payments of $180,000, at 85 cumulative payments of $720,000 and by 95 cumulative payments are $1,008,000.

In contrast, the File and Suspend strategy has Janet at 62 retiring and claiming her own reduced FRA benefit of $525 until FRA (that's $700 X .75 = $525). James at FRA files and suspends, then continues to work and accrue DRCs. At FRA Janet can now claim spousal benefits because James has filed and suspended his application. At FRA Janet claims spousal benefits on James's work record of $825 per month.

Here's how Janet's FRA spousal benefit is calculated. Janet's spousal benefit is half of James FRA benefit ($1,000) less her FRA benefit ($700) for a $300 spousal benefit (That's $1,000 -$700 = $300). Janet's FRA spousal benefit is added to her early retirement benefit for a total or $825 ($525 + $300).

At 70 total cumulative payments for the File and Suspend strategy are $71,100. At 70 James re-applies and claims benefits that include DRCs that boost his monthly payment to $2,640 (a 32 percent increase) and Janet continues to claim spousal benefits of $825. James and Janet receive a monthly payment of $3,465. By 85 the cumulative total for the couple is $694,800 and by 95 cumulative payments are $1,110,600.

Table 6.2 Early Retirement File and Suspend Strategy Break-Even Age

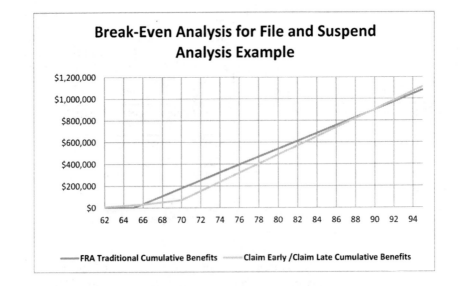

Table 6.2 is a graph of the comparison described in Table 6.1. Table 6.2 also illustrates the break-even age for scenario illustrated in Table 6.1. The

break-even age for the scenario in Table 6.1 is around 90 years-old. When selecting an optimal claiming strategy the break-even age plays a major role in decision-making. To take full advantage of the file and suspend approach you should expect to live a long life after the break-even age.

Applying for Benefits at FRA or Later is Often to Key to Maximization

On the surface the following File and Suspend Combo approach may seem like an unworkable approach. What makes this a viable approach is the age of the spouse. The spouse must be FRA to apply for spousal benefits only and to be eligible to later claim benefits on his or her own work record. (Or to start by claiming benefits on his or her own work record, then later switch to spousal benefits.) *It is important to note that this option is not allowed if the spouse applies for either benefit prior to FRA.*

Many individuals and couples try to develop their own unique claiming strategies. When creating an unusual strategy there many rules to keep in mind. The following Social Security rules are at the top of the list:

- ❖ Both spouses cannot claim benefits at the same time.
- ❖ One spouse must apply for benefits, in order for the other FRA spouse to be able to claim spousal benefits. (Remember, you can always file and suspend.)
- ❖ An eligible FRA spouse can apply for spousal benefits only, work to accrue DRCs, and switch to his or her own account.
- ❖ Always determine the break-even point of your strategy. As a couple you should plan to enjoy life after the break-even point.

Restricted Application and the File and Suspend Combo Example

The file and suspend approach works best for married couples if one has little or no Social Security benefits of their own. For couples that have similar earnings records a combination approach may provide the optimal claiming strategy. The following is a File and Suspend Combo Strategy example that details the procedure for a FRA couple that plans to work until age 70. Table 6.3 provides a side-by-side comparison of the Traditional Approach and the File and Suspend Combo Approach. This section concludes with Table 6.4 which indicates that the break-even age for File and Suspend Combo Strategy is 80 years old.

Table 6.3 is a side-by-side comparison of the Traditional Approach and the File and Suspend Combo Strategy for FRA claimants.

1. *Ken and Amy are both FRA and plan to work until they are 70 years old. Ken's FRA benefit is $2,000. Amy's FRA benefit is $850.*
2. *At age 66 Ken files and suspends. Amy can now file for spousal benefits of $1,000 per month on Ken's earning's record.*

3. *When FRA Amy applies for spousal benefits. Amy immediately files a "restricted application" for spousal benefits only. (This way she can switch to her own earnings record at age 70. If Amy does not file a restricted application for spousal benefits the SSA will automatically assume that she is claiming her own benefits and not accumulating DRCs.*

4. *Ken works until 70 years old and re-applies for benefits. Ken's benefits have increased 8 percent per year for four years ($2,000 X 1.32 = $2,640). Due to Ken's DRCs his monthly benefit is now $2,640.*

5. *At 70 years-old Amy switches from spousal benefits to benefits from her own work record. DRCs have increased Amy's benefits by 32 percent ($850 X 1.32 = $1,122.00). (The spousal benefit is terminated.)*

6. *To sum it up, at age 70, Ken and Amy each claim benefits on their own work records for a total of $3,762 per month.*

For the Traditional Approach at FRA Ken claims his FRA benefit and Amy claims her FRA spousal benefit a for monthly payment of $3,000. Cumulative payments are $180,000 at 70, $720,000 at 85 and $1,080,000 at 95.

The File and Suspend Approach shows how at FRA Ken files and suspends. This allows FRA Amy to file a "restricted application" for *spousal benefits only* of $1,000 per month. (This is the combo part of the plan.) Ken and Amy continue to work and accrue DRCs. At 70 Ken re-applies for benefits that have now increased by 32 percent. Amy stops her spousal benefit and claims benefits on her own work record. While FRA Amy worked from 66 to 70 she accrued DRCs that increases her own FRA benefit by 32 percent. Amy can now claim a benefit that is $122 per month greater than her spousal benefit. Here's the calculation, that's $1,122 (increased FRA benefit) - $1,000 (spousal benefit) = $122 increase in benefits. To sum it up, at 70 the file and suspend combo strategy has cumulative payments of $60,000, at 85 cumulative payments are $769,560, and at 95 total cumulative payments are $1,242,600.

The example in Table 6.3 is complex. If after trying several approaches you discover that the File and Suspend Combo Strategy is the optimal approach for your personal financial situation, I suggest verifying your implementation plan with a financial professional and a representative from the SSA. Rules change, employment lay-offs, re-organizations, or expected benefits could be negatively impacted by the Government Offset Provision (GOP) or Windfall Elimination Provision (WEP) (for details see Chapter 8: What Could Reduce Your Benefits). It is important to have all the details in-hand before embarking on a long-term plan.

Table 6.3 Side-by-Side Comparisons of the Traditional Approach and the File and Suspend Combo Strategy for a Married FRA Couple

Traditional Approach Ken Draws 100% at 66, and Amy Draws 50% Spousal Benefit age 66	File and Suspend Combo Approach At 66 FRA Ken Files and Suspends, at FRA Amy applies for Spousal Benefits Only on a Restricted Application. At 70 Ken and Amy both apply for Benefits with DRCs (132% of their FRA Benefits) on their own Work Records
At 66, Ken files for payments of $2,000 per month. Amy draws 50% of Ken's benefits as spousal payments of $1,000 per month. The couple receives a total of $3,000 per month.	At 66, Ken "Files and Suspends" and continues to work. Ken's File and Suspend application allows Amy to claim for FRA spousal benefits of $1,000 per month. Amy files a "Restricted Application" for spousal benefits only. This allows Amy to continue to work and accrue DRCs and file on her own work record.
At 70 total cumulative payments = **$180,000**	At 70 total cumulative payments = **$60,000**
At 70 no action	At age 70 Ken re-files for benefits of $2,640 per month ($2,000 X 1.32 = $2,640). At age 70 Amy switches to her own work record ($850 X 1.32 = $1,122). The couple's total monthly benefit is $3,942.
At 85 total payments = **$720,000**	At 85 payments = **$769,560**
At 95 total payments = **$1,008,000**	At 95 payments = **$1,242,600**
First death survivor receives $2,000 per month	First death survivor receives $2,640 per month

Note: This example does not include Cost-Of-Living Adjustments (COLAs), Medicare deductions, or other adjustments.

Table 6.4 below indicates that the break-even age for Ken and Amy is about 80. Table 6.4 shows how the Traditional Approach provides more benefits before age 80. After age 80 the File and Suspend Combo approach provides more benefits. Therefore your longevity will play an important role if you select this type of claiming strategy.

Table 6.4 File and Suspend Combo Example

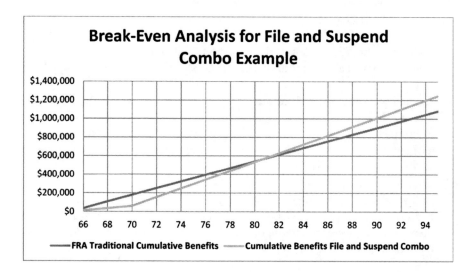

If after FRA you continue to work but cannot complete your plan of working until age 70, you can still file for benefits anytime between FRA and 70. There are no government imposed penalties for not reaching your personal financial goal.

CHAPTER 7: HOW WORKING AFTER RETIREMENT CAN INCREASE YOUR BENEFITS

The "Working after FRA Retirement Strategy" works best for:

❖ individuals that have years where they didn't make any income or made very little income.

❖ people who want to increase their monthly benefit.

❖ folks who have small or no retirement savings.

According to the SSA, working beyond your full retirement age (FRA) will allow you to increase your monthly benefit in two ways:

1. Each year you work adds another year of earnings to your Social Security record. Higher lifetime earnings may mean higher benefits when you retire. The Automatic Earnings Reappraisal Operation (AERO) is a computer operation that reexamines earnings not previously considered in the original appraisal of your work record.

    If the worker's earning's for the year are higher than the earnings that were used in the original benefit computation, the SSA substitutes the new year of earnings. The higher the earnings, the more your "re-figured benefit might be".

    AERO is run twice a year, usually in late October and the following March. The payments reflecting the increased benefits are issued in December and May. For more information about this process see "How Work Affects Your Benefits" available online at the SSA Web site located at www.socialsecurity.gov/pubs/10069.html.

2. Your benefit will automatically increase by a certain percentage from the time you reach your full retirement age until you start receiving your benefits or until you reach age 70 (see Table 5.1). This is called Delayed Retirement Credits (DRCs) and the annual percentage of increase varies depending on your year of birth. For example, if you were born in 1943 or later, the SSA adds eight percent per year to your benefit for each year that you delay claiming Social Security benefits beyond your FRA.

Key Benefits for Working after Your FRA

If you work beyond FRA there are two primary things that you need to take into consideration:

❖ If you decide to delay your retirement, be sure to sign up for Medicare at age 65. In some circumstances, medical insurance costs more if you delay applying for it. More information about Medicare at the SSA Web site in a publication titled, "A Word about Medicare" located in the center of the Web page at www.socialsecruity.gov/pubs/1077.html#a0=6 .

❖ The SSA benefit increases no longer apply when you reach age 70, even if you continue to delay taking benefits.

For example, let's say that you turn 70 in February 2012. If you earn $4,520 in January 2012 you can get the maximum ($1,130 X 4 = $4,520) number of credits for 2012. All your earnings after February 2012 are not included in SSA benefit calculations.

How Big of an Impact Will Working After Retirement Have on Benefits?

Your Social Security benefits are based on your top 35 years of earnings and not need. If the earner continues to work he or she can "backfill" earlier work years and increase monthly benefits. Every year the SSA reviews each claimants work record. If the latest year's earnings are one of your 35 highest earnings years, the SSA recalculates your benefits and increases your monthly benefit. *This is an automatic process and does not require any activity on your part.* On the other hand, it is not a speedy process. The SSA provides this example, in December 2012; you should receive an increase based on your 2011 earnings if those earnings increased your benefit. The increase is retroactive to January 2012.

Your Social Security benefit is based on 35 of your highest earning years. Let's say that you have two "off-the-charts" earning years after your retirement. Each year gets equal weight. Therefore two years out of 35 years is 2/35 = .057. If your monthly Social Security check is $2,400, the impact will be an increase of .057 X $2,400 = $137 (rounded) per month or $1,644 per year.

Your Birth Year and the Amount of Your Delayed Benefit

Table 7.1 shows how working past your FRA can increase your monthly benefit. The automatic amount of increase for working past your FRA is based on the year of your birth. Just like the birth years of different people, the yearly rate of increase changes from year to year. The current DRC increase is 8 percent per year. For a more precise calculation use Table 7.1 and locate your birth year to determine the exact amount of annual and monthly increases.

Table 7.1 Increase in Delayed Social Security Benefits by Year of Birth

Increase for Delayed Retirement		
Year of Birth	Yearly Rate of Increase	Monthly Rate of Increase
1933-1934	5.50%	11/24 of 1%
1935-1936	6.00%	1/2 of 1%
1937-1938	6.50%	13/24 of 1%
1939-1940	7.00%	7 1/2 of 1%
1941-1942	7.50%	5/8 of 1%
1943 or later	8.00%	2/3 of1%
Note: If you were born on January 1st, you should refer to the rate of increase for the previous year.		

Source: Social Security Administration, (www.ssa.gov), 2012.

For example, Jeff worked for 22 years in private industry and four years had no earnings when he returned to school. After graduating he started to work again and replaced the zeros with considerably higher numbers. Jeff plans to continue to work until he is near 70 years-old and expects to replace some of his lower-earning years with his higher earnings.

A Warning for Early Retirees Who Plan to Continue Working

According to *Kiplinger* magazine (McCormally, May 2011) about 250,000 Social Security claimants forfeited $757 million in benefits in the first seven months of 2009. The amount forfeited is a 14 percent increase for the same period in 2008 when about $666 million in Social Security benefits was relinquished.

The financial crisis of 2008 may have played a role in the amount of forfeited benefits. However, applying for early Social Security benefits and working is a bad mix for your long-term financial well-being.

How Much Can Your Earn While Receiving Social Security Benefits?

Taxation and Social Security benefits were discussed in Chapter 1: Increasing Your Benefits by Selecting the "Right" Application Date in the section titled, "Taxation of Social Security Retirement Benefits for Early Retirees". The following are a few general questions and answers that are important:

- ❖ How much can you earn while receiving Social Security retirement benefits? Early retirees can earn $14,640 a year and not lose any benefits in 2012.
- ❖ For early retirees, the SSA will deduct $1 in benefits for every $2 earned above $14,640.
- ❖ The same earnings limits apply to a child or spouse who works and receives benefits on your record

Earnings for a beneficiary who in their FRA year are as follows:
- ❖ Can earn $38,880 a year and not lose any benefits in 2012.
- ❖ The SSA will deduct $1 for every $3 earned above $38,880.
- ❖ The same earnings limits apply to a child or spouse who works and receives benefits on your record

After the full-retirement year Social Security claimants can earn as much as they want without any loss of benefits.

How Unemployment Benefits Affect Your Social Security Benefits

According to the SSA, unemployment insurance benefits are not counted under the Social Security regulations as earned income. Therefore unemployment does not affect your receipt of Social Security benefits. However, the unemployment benefit amount of an individual may be reduced by the receipt of a pension or other retirement income, including Social Security and Railroad Retirement benefits. If there is a reduction, the reduction is applied by the state unemployment department to the unemployment benefit.

In some states, the rules for collecting unemployment benefits and Social Security retirement benefits at the same time change from time to time. (For example, in Virginia the rules have changed three times from July 2003 to July 2011). You should contact your state unemployment office for information on how (or if) your state applies the reduction. For the latest information about your unemployment insurance status refer online to Career One Stop located at www.servicelocator.org/OWSLinks.asp. However, before taking any action you should talk with a representative from your local unemployment office.

CHAPTER EIGHT: WHAT COULD REDUCE YOUR BENEFITS?

There are several elements that can reduce your expected benefit, discover if the following applies to you:
- ❖ integration of benefits with other retirement plans
- ❖ government pension offsets (GPOs)
- ❖ Windfall Elimination Provision (WEP).

Individuals can download their personal Social Security Statements from the Internet at www.ssa.gov/mystatement/. The estimated amount of benefits listed on the statement may be overstated if you have a pension from employment that did not pay Social Security taxes. However, if you receive a pension from an organization where you paid Social Security taxes your social security benefit will not be reduced.

If you worked for a place where you did not pay Social Security taxes (such as a school district, police or fire department, local, state or federal government agency) you may be entitled to a civil service pension. You may also be entitled to a spousal or widow(er) s Social Security benefit based on your spouse's work record. If you are due a spousal or survivor's benefit you may lose a portion of your Social Security benefit due to your government pension.

CAUTION: This reduction is not listed on your Social Security statement and can be potentially harmful to your financial health.

This chapter covers many of the rules that affect government and private pensions and how these rules are important when calculating your future retirement income. Being aware of these rules may affect your decision-making for Social security benefits and determining which pension is best for your long-term financial retirement plan. .

Understanding Integrated Pension Plans

An integrated pension plan is defined as a plan that associates your pension benefits with you Social Security benefits. The perception of many individuals is that retirement pensions with integrated pension plans are trying to lower their employee retirement planning costs. However, in many cases the integrated pension plan is geared towards a reaching pre-determined benefit amount using pension and Social Security benefits.

Integrated pension plans deduct Social Security benefits from earned pension benefits in a qualified pension plan. However, this offset or reduction is limited due to tax reform legislation passed in the 80's. The Tax Reform Act states that employers cannot reduce benefits provided by the integrated retirement plan by more than 50 percent. Therefore if the Social Security benefits and pension benefits are combined but exceed the targeted goal, the pension amount cannot be further reduced.

The following is an example of how this works. The annual Social Security FRA benefit for Carol is $8,000. The annual pension for Carol is $10,000. The employer can cut the pension amount by 50 percent of the annual Social Security benefit (in this example, $4,000). In other words, the $4,000 deduction is 50 Percent of the $8,000 Annual Social Security amount. Therefore the employer would pay $6,000. (That is, the $10,000 pension less the $4,000 Social Security amount which equals $6,000.) Therefore Carol's integrated pension play would be $14,000 per year. (This includes Carol's $8,000 annual FRA Social Security benefit and $6,000 per year for her pension).

Defining Government Pension Offsets (GPO) s and Social Security Benefits

The Government Pension Offset (GPO) started in 1977 and applies to all retiree's whose spouses are eligible for Social Security. As a general rule, individuals who complete 40 work credits are eligible for Social Security retirement benefits. Spouses who have not worked or who have less than 40 work credits are eligible for spousal Social Security retirement benefits. The GPO reduces spousal and widow(er) Social Security benefits according to a pre-determined formula.

The GPO applies to individuals who receive a pension not covered by Social Security. This is called an "uncovered pension". Often individuals with an uncovered pension are eligible for Social Security benefits as a spouse or widow(er).

Note: The SSA will not offset Social Security benefits if the uncovered pensions are from the Veteran's Administration, the Railroad Board, or from other countries.

A Practical Example of How GPO Works

If you receive benefits on your spouse's earnings record and you also receive a pension for your work that was not covered by Social Security, your monthly benefits may be affected by your pension and you may be subject to a reduction in benefits. This type of Social Security benefit reduction is called a Government Pension Offset (GPO). For more information see "The Government Pension Offset Fact Sheet located at www.socialsecruity.gov/pubs/10007.html"

Under the GPO, the SSA may reduce your spousal or widow(er) benefit. (For more information see www.socialsecurity.gov/retire2/gpo.htm.). For example, let's say that the husband has a Social Security benefit of $1,800 per month and the wife has a state agency pension of $2,400 per month. The GPO will reduce her spousal benefits to zero. The following are step-by-step directions for calculating the GPO reduction:

1. Wife's Social Security spousal benefits $900 (as stated on the husband's annual Social Security Statement).
2. Wife's government benefit of $2,400.
3. Calculation of GPO for spousal benefit, $900 – 2/3 ($2,400) = $900-$1,600 = <$0.
4. The Social Security Spousal benefit is reduced to **zero**.

Let the Internet Do the Math For You

The SSA provides an online calculator that can assist you in calculating the amount of the GPO for your personal financial position. The online calculator is located at the SSA Web page titled, "The Government Pension Offset Calculator" at www.socialsecurity.gov/retire2/gpo-calc.htm. The online calculator is specifically designed to assist you in estimating your Social Security benefit for work not covered by Social Security.

The Government Pension Offset (GPO) unlike the Windfall Elimination Provision (WEP) also applies to widow(er)s and survivors who have pensions based on his or work in government employment (that is not covered by Social Security). In this situation, the GPO-affected widow(er) benefit is calculated in the same manner as the example above. Generally, this offset reduces the widow(er) or survivor benefit to zero and there isn't an optimal claiming strategy.

Using the above example, let's look at the husband's benefits. There is no offset if the husband receives a dependent's benefit from his spouse's government pension. The husband's receipt of a benefit from his spouse's government pension will not affect how much he receives from Social Security.

GOP Exemptions

Of course, there are some folks that are exempt from the GOP. For example, if you receive a government pension that is not based on earnings you may be exempt. To discover if you qualify for an exemption see www.socialsecurity.gov/pubs/10007.html#a0=3&when=.

Windfall Elimination Provisions and Social Security Benefits

The Windfall Elimination Provision (WEP) was established in 1983. It was designed to remove the unintended advantages that the weighting of the regular Social Security formula would otherwise provide for persons who have substantial pensions from uncovered employment. In other words, Social Security uses a non-linear formula to make payments progressive. The progressive formula provides a higher replacement income for low earners.

For example, let's say that an individual has a high government pension but 10 percent of his career earnings were in consulting for which he paid Social Security taxes. For the purposes of Social Security this would make him or her appear to be a low earner and someone who needed higher benefit relative to earnings for low income.

WEP affects how the SSA calculates Social Security retirement or disability benefits if someone receives a pension from work not covered by Social Security. (For details see the Social Security WEP page located at www.socialsecurity.gov/retire2/wep.htm). WEP recognizes that individuals can have retirement benefits that are not covered by Social Security and benefits that are covered by Social Security.

Additionally, someone may qualify for Social Security spousal benefits. Therefore Social Security may reduce both types of benefits using the Windfall Elimination Provision (WEP) *and* the Government Offset Provision (GPO). For example, an individual may have a retirement benefit subject to WEP and a spouse's benefit that is subject to GPO. Note: Windfall Elimination Provisions do not apply to survivors.

Calculating the WEP Reduced Benefit

If you receive pensions not "covered" by Social Security and are eligible for Social Security retirement benefits on your own earnings record or your spouse's earnings record the SSA provides an online calculator. The online WEP calculation for determining the amount of your Social Security benefit after the WEP deduction is at www.ssa.gov/retire2/anyPiaWepjs04.htm.

By the way, none of the SSA calculators are linked to your earnings record. Each calculator is dependent on the information you enter. If you enter incorrect estimated earnings amounts, then your estimated benefits will be wrong. Additionally, all calculators assume that you have enough work credits. There are two versions of the WEP calculator:

❖ One version indicates the effect of WEP on your estimated benefits.
❖ The second calculator is the detailed version and must be downloaded and installed on your computer. The detailed version of the WEP calculator provides the most precise estimates of the two calculators.

Limits on WEP Reductions

According to the SSA the Windfall Elimination Provisions (WEP) reduces your eligibility year benefit before it is reduced or increased due to early retirement, DRCs, COLAs or other factors. If you are 62 in 2012 and have 20 years of substantial earnings WEP will reduce your monthly benefit by $383.50. Let's say your monthly wages are $2,000. For a worker who turns 62 in 2012 the WEP rules are:

1. The first $767 in wages is multiplied by 0.9
2. The next $3,857 is multiplied by 0.32
3. The remaining wages are multiplied by 0.15
4. The sum of the total equals the monthly payment amount:
$$(\$767 \times 0.9) + ((\$3,857 - \$767) \times 0.32) + (\$0 \times 0.15) =$$
$$\$690.30 + \$988.80 = \$1,924.70$$
The worker is entitled to a benefit of **$1,679.10**

This formula assumes that the worker has completed 30 years of "substantial earnings". Table 8.1 illustrates the percentage factor used in the application of WEP. Let's say that the example retiree only has 20 years of substantial earnings. The calculation would be modified as follows:
1. The first $767 in wages is multiplied by 0.4
2. The next $3,857 is multiplied by 0.32
3. The remaining by 0.15
4. The sum of the total equals the monthly payment amount:
$$(\$767 \times 0.4) + ((\$3,857 - \$767) \times 0.32) + (\$0 \times 0.15) =$$
$$\$306.80 + \$988.80 = \textbf{\$1,295.60}$$
The maximum amount of reduction is as follows:
$1,679.10 - $1,295.60 = $383.50

There is a limit on the amount that your benefit can be reduced. Table 8.1 shows the maximum amount of reduction for your retirement year. The column on the far left indicates your eligibility year. That is when you turn 62.

Table 8.1 Maximum WEP Reduction by Eligibility Year

	Years of Substantial Earnings									
20 or less	21	22	23	24	25	26	27	28	29	30
1990	$178.00	$160.20	$142.40	$124.60	$106.80	$89.00	$71.20	$53.40	$35.60	$17.80
1991	185	166.5	148	129.5	111	92.5	74	55.5	37	18.5
1992	193.5	174.2	154.8	135.5	116.1	96.8	77.4	58.1	38.7	19.4
1993	200.5	180.5	160.4	140.4	120.3	100.3	80.2	60.2	40.1	20.1
1994	211	189.9	168.8	147.7	126.6	105.5	84.4	63.3	42.2	21.1
1995	213	191.7	170.4	149.1	127.8	106.5	85.2	63.9	42.6	21.3
1996	218.5	196.7	174.8	153	131.1	109.3	87.4	65.6	43.7	21.9
1997	227.5	204.8	182	159.3	136.5	113.8	91	68.3	45.5	22.8
1998	238.5	214.7	190.8	167	143.1	119.3	95.4	71.6	47.7	23.9
1999	252.5	227.3	202	176.8	151.5	126.3	101	75.8	50.5	25.3
2000	265.5	239	212.4	185.9	159.3	132.8	106.2	79.7	53.1	26.6
2001	280.5	252.5	224.4	196.4	168.3	140.3	112.2	84.2	56.1	28.1
2002	296	266.4	236.8	207.2	177.6	148	118.4	88.8	59.2	29.6
2003	303	272.7	242.4	212.1	181.8	151.5	121.2	90.9	60.6	30.3
2004	306	275.4	244.8	214.2	183.6	153	122.4	91.8	61.2	30.6
2005	313.5	282.2	250.8	219.5	188.1	156.8	125.4	94.1	62.7	31.4
2006	328	295.2	262.4	229.6	196.8	164	131.2	98.4	65.6	32.8
2007	340	306	272	238	204	170	136	102	68	34
2008	355.5	320	284.4	248.9	213.3	177.8	142.2	106.7	71.1	35.6
2009	372	334.8	297.6	260.4	223.2	186	148.8	111.6	74.4	37.2
2010	380.5	342.5	304.4	266.4	228.3	190.3	152.2	114.2	76.1	38.1
2011	374.5	337.1	299.6	262.2	224.7	187.3	149.8	112.4	74.9	37.5
2012	383.5	345.2	306.8	268.5	230.1	191.8	153.4	115.1	76.7	38.4

Important: The maximum amount may be overstated. The WEP reduction is limited to one-half of your pension from non-covered employment.

SOURCE: Social Security Administration (www.ssa.gov), 2012.

WEP, Retirement Planning and Maximizing Your Benefits

According to the SSA your monthly benefits increase or decrease based on your age at retirement. Therefore age at retirement and the WEP reduction can have unexpected results. Let's say that Mike's FRA benefit is $1,000 per month (after his WEP reduction).

❖ **Early Retirement:** Mike takes early retirement and receives 75 percent of his FRA benefit ($750 per month). If Mike has only 20 years of "substantial earnings" his benefit will be reduced by $383.50 (see Table 8.1). If Mike's FRA benefit had not been reduces by WEP, the benefit would have been $1,031. Early retirement changed the reduction. Early retirement **lowered** the reduction for WEP from $380.50 to $281.

❖ **Delayed Retirement:** Mike turned 66 in 2011. He plans to work until age 70. Mike's FRA benefit is $1,000 (after the WEP reduction). If Mike works until he is 70 the monthly benefit will be $1,320 (an 8 percent increase per year for four years). If Mike's FRA benefit had not been reduced by WEP his DRC benefit would have been $1,815. Delaying retirement **increased** Mike's WEP reduction from $380.50 (see Table 8.1) to $495 (rounded).

When you have your personal Social Security statement (which you can download at www.socialsecurity.gov/mystatement/) you can use the online SSA calculator to experiment with different strategies and retirement dates. For example, you can determine the impact of your WEP deduction and proposed retirement date by using the online WEP calculator at the SSA Web site www.socialsecurity.gov/retire2/anyPiaWepjs04.htm/.

Note: One maximizing strategy for couples affected by WEP is for the high earner spouse to delay retirement and receive spousal benefits from the lower earner spouse's "non-covered" pension while the pension owner collects payments.

CHAPTER 9: CONCLUSION

In this chapter you'll find:
- ❖ how to monitor changes in SSA regulations
- ❖ sources for additional Social Security information and materials

How to Monitor Changes in SSA Regulations

The following are several resources that are helpful in monitoring changes in Social Security.

The Social Security Administration has developed an agency wide plan, titled, "The Agency Strategic Plan: Security Value for Americans, Fiscal Years 2012-2016" located at http://www.socialsecurity.gov/asp/plan-2013-2016.pdf.

The U.S. House of Representatives Ways and Means Subcommittee on Social Security is responsible for bills and matters referred to the Committee that relate to the Federal Old Age, Survivor's and Disability Insurance System, the Railroad Retirement System, and the employment taxes and trust fund operations relating to those systems. The Committee also oversees bills and matters involving Title II of the Social Security Act and Chapter 22 of the Internal Revenue Code (the Railroad Retirement Tax Act). In addition to provisions in Title VII and XI of the Act relating to procedure and administration involving the Old Age, Survivors and Disability System (http://waysandmeans.house.gov/Subcommittees/Subcommittee/?IssueID=4772.)

Sources for Additional Information

The following is an abbreviated list of sources for additional reading. At this time all the sources listed available free and downloadable online.

Retirement Benefits
"When to Start Receiving Benefits"
www.ssa.gov/pubs/10147.pdf

"Retirement Benefits"
www.ssa.gov/pubs/10035.pdf

"How Work Affects Your Benefits"
www.ssa.gov/pubs/10069.pdf

Benefits for Children
"Benefits for Children"
www.ssa.gov/pubs/100085.pdf

Family Benefits
"What Your Need to Know When You Get Retirement or Survivor Benefits"
www.ssa.gov/pubs/10077.pdf

Benefits for Survivors
"Benefits for Survivors"
www.ssa.gov/pubs/10084.html/10084.pdf

Benefits for Women
"Benefits for Women"
www.ssa.gov/pubs/10127.pdf

APPENDIX A

A COMPARISON OF THE RESTRICTED APPLICATION AND FILE AND SUSPEND MAXIMIZATION APPROACHES

The following are comparisons of maximization strategies matched to the Traditional claiming strategy. Specific claiming strategies used are the Restricted Application methodology and File and Suspend strategy for a couple claiming early benefits, FRA benefits and DRCs benefits. Overall, Appendix A illustrates how working longer maximizes social security payments.

It is important to keep in mind that there are many combinations of strategies available. That's why online Social Security benefit optimization calculators or software programs are so important. For more information about online calculators and programs see Chapter 5: "Claim Now and Claim More Later" to Boost Benefits.

The example couple used in Appendix A shows how different approaches, at different times, have different outcomes. All the figures in Appendix A use the same basic information, then apply different claiming strategies at various times to determine which approach provides an optimal outcome. The limited number of comparisons provided the following results:

❖ Traditional Approach: Cumulative payments at 95: $1,080,000.

❖ Case A: File and Suspend with Anne taking early retirement and Henry delaying retirement. Cumulative payments at 95: $1,129,680.

❖ Case B: Restricted Application with Anne taking early retirement and Henry delaying retirement. Cumulative payments at 95: $1,082,880.

❖ Case C: File and Suspend with Anne taking retirement at FRA and Henry delaying retirement. (**The Optimal Strategy for Henry and Anne.**) Cumulative payments at 95: $1,152,000.

❖ Case D: Restricted Application with Anne taking retirement at FRA and Henry delaying retirement. Cumulative payments at 95: $1,130,880.

Table A.1: The Traditional Claiming Strategy

Traditional Claiming Strategy Henry, FRA 66, $2,000 Anne FRA 66, $800	Monthly Amount	Months	Total
Henry **files** at FRA, 66	$2,000		
Anne, 66 files for spousal benefits on Henry's work record	$1,000		
Cumulative Payments at 70	$3,000	60	$180,000
Payments from 70 to 85	$3,000	180	$540,000
Payments from 85 to 95	$3,000	120	$360,000
Cumulative Payments at 95	$3,000	360	$1,080,000
First death survivor amount			$2,000

TableA.2: Graphic Display of the Traditional Claiming Strategy

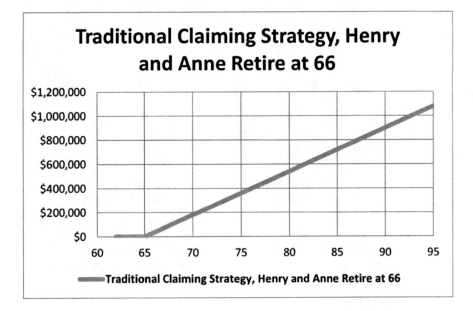

Table A.1 shows the Traditional claiming strategy. A couple, Henry and Anne plan to retire at FRA 66. "Dual Entitlement" allows Anne to draw $800 on her on her own earning's record or claim 50 percent of Henry's benefit as a spousal benefit ($1,000). Anne claims her FRA benefit of $1,000 and Henry claims his FRA benefit of $2,000 for a total of $3,000 per month.

Table A.2 graphically illustrates the cumulative payments Henry and Anne will receive until 95. If the couple retires at FRA using the Traditional approach by 95 they will receive $1,080,000 in retirement benefits.

The File and Suspend Early Retirement Compared to the Traditional Plan

Table A.3 shows the cumulative payments for Henry and Anne if they use the File and Suspend Early Retirement approach (Case A). Table A.4 graphically shows that the File and Suspend Early Retirement approach doesn't break-even with the Traditional method until age 85. After 85 the File and Suspend approach has a higher yield than the Traditional method.

Table A.3: File and Suspend Early Retirement Strategy Case A

Case A Henry, FRA 66, $2,000 Anne FRA 66, $800			
	Monthly Amount	**Months**	**Total**
Henry **files and suspends** at FRA, 66	$0		
At 62, Anne files for reduced spousal benefits on Henry's work record	$750		
Cumulative Payments at 70	$750	96	$72,000
At 70 Henry draws his own benefits with DRCs of 32% ($2,640), Anne continues to draw reduced spousal benefits ($750)			
Payments from 70 to 85	$3,390	192	$650,880 $722,880
Payments from 85 to 95	$3,390	120	$406,800
Cumulative Payments at 95			$1,129,680
First death survivor amount			**$2,640**

Table A.4 illustrates how Case A the File and Suspend Early Retirement approach compares with the Traditional method of claiming retirement benefits.

Table A4: Break-Even Analysis of Traditional Strategy and Case A

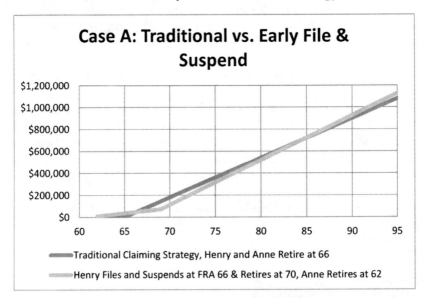

Case A: Traditional vs. Early File & Suspend

Traditional Claiming Strategy, Henry and Anne Retire at 66
Henry Files and Suspends at FRA 66 & Retires at 70, Anne Retires at 62

Table A.5: Restricted Application and Early Retirement Case B

Case B Henry, FRA 66, $2,000 Anne FRA 66, $800	Monthly Amount	Months	Total
Anne files for early retirement at 62	$600	48	$28,800
Henry at FRA, files for spousal benefits on Anne's work record using **a restricted application**	$300		
Cumulative Payments when Henry is 70	$900	48	$43,200
At 70 Henry draws his own benefits with DRCs of 32% ($2,640), Anne continues to draw reduced benefits on her own record ($600)			
Payments from 70 to 85	$3,240	192	$622,080 **$694,080**
Payments from 85 to 95	$3,240	120	$388,800
Cumulative Payments at 95			**$1,082,880**
First death survivor amount			**$2,640**

Table A.5 shows Case B the Early Retirement Restricted Application method. Anne can take early retirement at 62. This allows Henry at FRA to claim spousal benefits on Anne's work record while he accrues DRCs. Henry retires at age 70 with a 32 percent increase in benefits and four years of "free spousal" benefits. The DRCs that Henry accrues will increase his monthly benefit and the first death survivor amount.

Table A.6: Break-Even Analysis for Early Retirement Case B

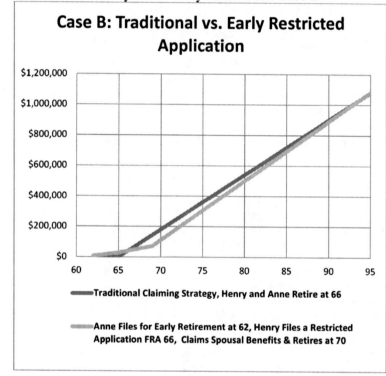

Table A.6 illustrates that by age 95 the cumulative payments for the Traditional approach and the Early Restricted Application approach are almost the same. Therefore the chief benefit of this approach is Anne's early retirement at 62 as opposed to working until 66.

Case C is the Optimal Strategy for Henry and Anne. Table A.7 illustrates how Henry at FRA is Filing and Suspending so Anne can file for $1,000 of spousal benefits at 66. Henry continues to work and accrue DRCs increasing his benefit by 32 percent ($2,640). The break-even point for this strategy is after age 85. After 85 the couple receives more than the Traditional claiming strategy. By age 95 Henry and Anne will take over $100,000 more to the bank than if they used the Traditional claiming strategy. Additionally, their survivor benefit is 32 percent greater than it would have been if they had used the Traditional methodology.

This illustrates that each individual, couple, widow(er), or survivor has an optimal claiming strategy that matches their personal circumstances. Claiming strategies are complex. Researching claiming approaches and getting advice from a financial professional, lawyer, or CPA about the best way to implement a Social Security maximization plan can assist you in avoiding costly mistakes.

Table A.7: File and Suspend FRA Approach and Case C

Case C Henry, FRA 66, $2,000 Anne FRA 66, $800	Monthly Amount	Months	Total
Henry at FRA 66, **files and suspends**	$0		
Anne at FRA 66, files for spousal benefits on Henry's work record	$1,000		
Cumulative Payments at 70 At 70 Henry draws own benefits with DRCs that increase benefit by 32% ($2,640) Anne continue to draw $1,000 per month	$1,000	60	$60,000
Payments from 70 to 85	$3,640	192	$698,880 $758,880
Payments from 85 to 95	$3,640	120	$436,800
Cumulative Payments at 95			$1,195,680
First death survivor amount			$2,640

Table A.8: Case C File and Suspend FRA Break-Even Analysis

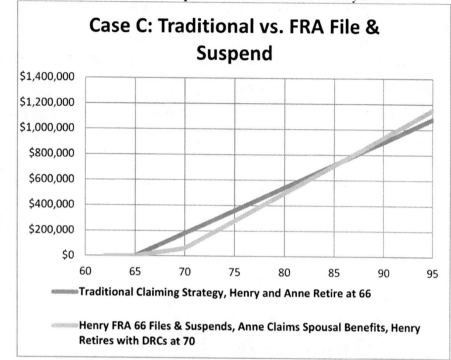

Table A.8 graphically illustrates how the Traditional claiming method compares to Case C the FRA File and Suspend approach. The break-even age for the two methods is around 85. Case C is the optimal approach and results in higher total cumulative payments by 95. However, if Henry and Anne do not expect to live past 85 this is not a good claiming strategy due to longevity risks.

Kathleen Sindell, Ph.D.

Table A.9: Case D FRA Restricted Application

Case D Henry, FRA 66, $2,000 Anne FRA 66, $800	Monthly Amount	Months	Total
Anne FRA 66 files for benefits	$800		
Henry FRA 66 files **Restricted Applciation** for spousal benefits on Anne's work record	$400		
Cumulative Payments at 70	$1,200	48	$57,600
At 70 Henry draws own benefits with DRCs (a 32% benefit increase) for $2,640 Anne continue to draw $600 per mo			
Payments from 70 to 85	$3,440	192	$660,480 $718,080
Payments from 85 to 95	$3,440	120	$412,800
Cumulative Payments at 95			$1,130,880
Firest death survivor amount			$2,640

Table A.9 illustrates Case D the FRA Restricted Application Strategy. At FRA 66 Anne claims her own benefits. Henry at FRA 66 files a Restricted Application, collects "free spousal benefits" on Anne's earning's record, and works until age 70. At age 70 Henry re-applies for benefits and has increased his monthly payment by 32 percent. The break-even age for this approach is 86. After age 86 Anne and Henry enjoy a higher cumulative return than if they used the Traditional Approach.

It is important to note that the cumulative payments for Case A and Case D are similar. What's the major difference in the two examples? In Case D the FRA Restricted Application Strategy, Anne works until FRA. In Case A the File and Suspend Early Retirement example, Anne takes early retirement. Therefore for decision-making purposes Case D does not favorably compare to Case A.

Table A.10 Break-Even Analysis for FRA Restricted Application Plan

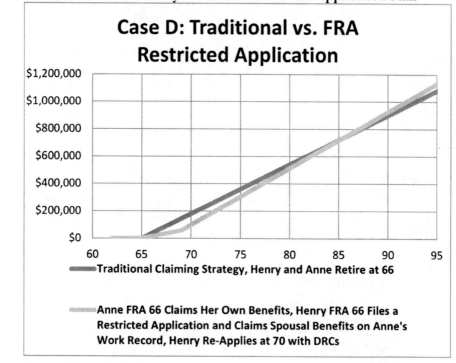

GLOSSARY

The Social Security Administration (SSA) located at
http://www.socialsecurity.gov/glossary.htm provides the following glossary
for individuals seeking a better understanding of the terms used by the SSA.

A

AIME (Average Indexed Monthly Earnings)
The dollar amount used to calculate your Social Security benefit if you
attained age 62 or became disabled (or died) after 1978. To arrive at your
AIME, we adjust your actual past earnings using an "average wage index," so
you won't lose the value of your past earnings (when money was worth more)
in relation to your more recent earnings. If you attained age 62 or became
disabled (or died) before 1978, we use Average Monthly Earnings (AME).

AME (Average Monthly Earnings)
The dollar amount used in calculating your monthly Social Security benefit if
you attained age 62 or became disabled (or died) before 1978. The AME is
determined by dividing the total earnings in the "computation years" by the
number of months in those same years.

B

Base Years
A worker's (wage earners) base years for computing Social Security benefits
are the years after 1950 up to the year of entitlement to retirement or
disability insurance benefits. For a survivor's claim, the base years include the
year of the worker's death.

Benefits
Social Security pays five types of benefits:
- ❖ Retirement
- ❖ Disability
- ❖ Family (dependents)
- ❖ Survivors
- ❖ Medicare

The retirement, family (dependents), survivor and disability programs pay
monthly cash benefits, and Medicare provides medical coverage.

Benefits – Reduced

You can get the following reduced monthly benefits before reaching full retirement age:

* Retirement benefits at age 62 through the month before your reach Full Retirement Age;

* Husband's or wife's benefits at age 62 through the month before you reach full retirement age, provided no child of your spouse either under age 18 or disabled and entitled to benefits is in your care;

* Widow's or widower's benefits beginning at any time from age 50 through the month before you reach full retirement age;

* Widow's or widower's benefits, if your spouse received a retirement benefit before full retirement age;

* Disability benefits received after a reduced retirement benefit; or

* Retirement or disability benefits received after a reduced widow's or widower's benefit. This applies only if you were born before 1928.

C

Child

We use the term "Child" to include your biological child or any other child who can inherit your personal property under State law or who meets certain specific requirements under the Social Security Act; such as:

* a legally adopted child,
* an equitably adopted child,
* a stepchild, or
* a grandchild.

Cost-Of-Living Adjustment (COLA)

Social Security benefits and Supplemental Security Income (SSI) payments may be automatically increased each year to keep pace with increases in the Cost-Of-Living (inflation).

Computation Years

Computation years are the years with highest earnings selected from the "base years." We add total earnings in the computation years and divide by the number of months in those years to get the AME or the AIME. (We use your 35 highest years of earnings to compute your retirement benefits.)

CPI-W (Consumer Price Index)

An index prepared by the U. S. Department of Labor that charts the rise in costs for selected goods and services. This index is used to compute Cost of living adjustments.

Credits (Social Security Credits)

Previously called "Quarters of Coverage". As you work and pay taxes, you earn credits that count toward your eligibility for future Social Security benefits. You can earn a maximum of four credits each year. Most people need 40 credits to qualify for benefits. Younger people need fewer credits to qualify for disability or survivors benefits.

D

Delayed Retirement Credits (DRC)

Social Security benefits are increased by a certain percentage (depending on date of birth) if a person delays taking retirement benefits beyond full retirement age. The benefit increase no longer applies after age 70, even if the person continues to delay taking benefits.

Dependent Benefits

See Family Benefits.

Direct Deposit

The standard way to receive Social Security benefits and Supplemental Security Income (SSI). Your money is sent electronically to an account in a financial institution (bank, trust company, savings and loan association, brokerage agency or credit union). For more information see Social Security Direct Deposit.

E

Early Retirement

You can start getting Social Security retirement benefits as early as age 62, but your benefit amount will be less than you would have gotten if you waited until your full retirement age.

If you take retirement benefits early, your benefit will remain permanently reduced, based on the number of months you received benefits before you reached full retirement age.

Early Retirement Age
Age 62. For more information read Retirement benefits by year of birth.

Earnings Record (lifetime record of earnings)
A chronological history of the amount of money you earned each year during your working lifetime. The credits you earned remain on your Social Security record even when you change jobs or have no earnings.

F

Family Benefits (Dependent Benefits)
When you're eligible for retirement or disability benefits, the following people may receive benefits on your record:

- ❖ spouse if he or she is at least 62 years old (or any age but caring for an entitled child under age 16 or disabled);
- ❖ children if they are unmarried and under age 18, or under age 19 and a full-time elementary or secondary student ;
- ❖ children age 18 or older but disabled before age 22;
- ❖ ex-spouses age 62 or older.

Family Maximum
The maximum amount of benefits payable to an entire family on any one worker's record.

FICA Tax
FICA stands for "Federal Insurance Contributions Act." It's the tax withheld from your salary or self-employment income that funds the Social Security and Medicare programs.

Full Retirement Age
The age at which a person may first become entitled to full or unreduced retirement benefits. For workers and spouses born in 1938 or later and widows/widowers born in 1940 or later, the retirement age increases gradually from age 65 until it reaches age 67 in the year 2022. This increase affects the amount of the reduction for persons who begin receiving reduced benefits. For more information see Full retirement age.

I

Insured Status
If you worked and earned enough Social Security credits to be eligible for retirement or disability benefits or enable your dependents to be eligible for benefits due to your retirement, disability, or death, you have insured status.

L

Lifetime Earnings "Earnings Record"
A chronological history of the amount of money you earned each year during your working lifetime. The credits you earned remain on your Social Security record even when you change jobs or have no earnings.

Lump Sum Death Payment
A one-time payment of $255 paid in addition to any monthly survivors benefits that are due. This benefit is paid only to your widow/widower or minor children.

M

Maximum Earnings
The maximum amount of earnings we can count in any calendar year when computing your Social Security benefit.

Medicare
See Health Insurance. For more information, see Medicare Resources and the Official U.S. Government Site for Medicare.

Month of Election
This usually applies to retirement claims. In certain situations, you can choose the month in which your benefits will start.

N

Normal Retirement Age
See Full Retirement Age.

Number Holder
See Wage Earner.

O

OASDI (Old Age Survivors and Disability Insurance)
The Social Security programs that provide monthly cash benefits to you and your dependents when you retire, to your surviving dependents, and to disabled workers and their dependents.

P

Payment Dates for Social Security Benefits
If you applied for Social Security benefits before May 1, 1997, your payments usually are dated and delivered on the 3rd of the month following the month for which the payment is due. For example, payments for January are delivered on February 3rd.

If the 3rd of the month is a Saturday, Sunday or Federal holiday, your payments are dated and delivered on the first day before the 3rd of the month which is not a Saturday, Sunday or Federal holiday. For example, if the 3rd is a Saturday or Sunday, payments are delivered on the preceding Friday.

If you filed for Social Security benefits May 1, 1997, or later, you are assigned one of three new payment days based on date of birth:

❖ If you were born on the -Your payment will be delivered on the...

❖ 1st through 10th of the month -Second Wednesday of the month

❖ 11th through 20th of the month - Third Wednesday of the month

❖ 21st through end of the month - Fourth Wednesday of the month

*If your scheduled Wednesday payment day is a Federal holiday, we'll send your payment on the preceding day that is not a Federal legal holiday.

Payment Dates for Supplemental Security Income (SSI) Payments
SSI payments are usually dated and delivered on the first day of the month for which they are due. However, if the first falls on a Saturday, Sunday or Federal holiday, they are dated and delivered on the first day preceding the first of the month which is not a Saturday, Sunday or Federal holiday.

PIA (Primary Insurance Amount)

The monthly amount payable if you are a retired worker who begins receiving benefits at full retirement age or if you're disabled and have never received a retirement benefit reduced for age.

Protective Filing Date

The date you first contact us about filing for benefits. It may be used to establish an earlier application date than when we receive your signed application.

Q

QC (Quarter of Coverage)

See Credits, (Social Security Credits).

R

Reduction Months

Months beginning with the first month you're entitled to reduced benefits up to, but not including, the month in which you reach full retirement age.

Representative Payee

If you receive Social Security benefits or Supplemental Security Income (SSI) and become unable to handle your own financial affairs, we (after a careful investigation) appoint a relative, a friend, or an interested party to handle your Social Security matters.

Representative payees are required to maintain complete accounting records and periodically provide reports to Social Security. For additional information see Representative Payee Program.

Retirement Age – Full Benefits

Full retirement age was 65 for many years. However, beginning with the year 2000 (for workers and spouses born in 1938 or later, or widows or widowers born in 1940 or later), the retirement age increases gradually from age 65 until it reaches age 67 in the year 2022.

Retirement Age – Minimum

The minimum age for retirement—age 62 for workers, and age 60 for widows or widowers. You can choose a reduced benefit any time before you reach full retirement age.

Retirement Earnings Test
If you receive monthly Social Security benefits before your full retirement age and work, your earnings from wages and/or self-employment cannot exceed a certain amount without reducing your monthly benefits.

Retroactive Benefits (Back Pay)
Monthly benefits that you may be entitled to before the month you actually apply, if you meet the requirements.

Retirement Benefit
Money that is payable to you upon retirement if you have enough Social Security credits.

S

Self-employment Income
You are self-employed if you operate a trade, business or profession, either individually or as a partner, and have net earnings of $400 or more in a taxable year.

Social Security
Social Security is based on a simple concept: While you work, you pay taxes into the Social Security system, and when you retire or become disabled, you, your spouse and your dependent children receive monthly benefits that are based on your reported earnings. Also, your survivors can collect benefits if you die.

Social Security Number (Social Security Card)
Your first and continuous link with Social Security is your nine-digit Social Security Number. It helps us to maintain an accurate record of your wages or self-employment earnings that are covered under the Social Security Act, and to monitor your record once you start getting Social Security benefits.

Social Security Office
Your local Social Security office is the place where you can:
- ❖ apply for a Social Security number;
- ❖ check on your earnings record;
- ❖ apply for Social Security benefits, Supplemental Security Income (SSI), and hospital insurance (Medicare) protection;
- ❖ enroll for medical insurance;
- ❖ get help applying for food stamps and;
- ❖ learn everything you need to know about your rights and obligations under the Social Security law.

There is no charge for any of our services. You can also call our toll-free telephone number, 1-800-772-1213, to receive all these services. Our TTY number is 1-800-325-0778. This toll-free telephone number service is available from 7 a.m. to 7 p.m. any business day. All calls are confidential. See our Social Security Office Locator for the address of your local office. In addition, many services are now available through the Internet

Spouse
You are the spouse of the worker if, when he or she applied for benefits:
- ❖ you and the worker were married; or
- ❖ you would have the status of a husband or a wife for that person's personal property if they had no will; or
- ❖ you went through a marriage ceremony in good faith, which would have been valid except for a legal impediment.

Supplemental Security Income (SSI)
A federal supplemental income program funded by general tax revenues (not Social Security taxes). It helps aged, blind, and disabled people who have limited income and resources by providing monthly cash payments to meet basic needs for food, clothing, and shelter. For more information, see Supplemental Security Income (SSI).

Survivors Benefits
Benefits based on your record (if you should die) are paid to your:
- ❖ widow/widower age 60 or older, 50 or older if disabled, or any age if caring for a child under age 16 or disabled before age 22
- ❖ children, if they are unmarried and under age 18, under 19 but still in school, or 18 or older but disabled before age 22; and
- ❖ parents if you provided at least one-half of their support.
- ❖ An ex-spouse could also be eligible for a widow/widower's benefit on your record. A special one-time lump sum payment of $255 may be made to your spouse or minor children.

W

Wage Earner
A person who earns Social Security credits while working for wages or self-employment income. Sometimes referred to as the "Number Holder" or "Worker."

Wages
All payment for services performed for an employer. Wages do not have to be cash. The cash value of all compensation paid to an employee in any form

other than cash is also considered wages, unless the form of payment is specifically not covered under the Social Security Act.

Widow
You are the widow/widower of the worker if, at the time the insured person died:
- ❖ you and the worker were validly married; or
- ❖ you would have the status of a husband or a wife for that person's personal property if he or she had no will; or
- ❖ you went through a marriage ceremony in good faith that would have been valid except for a legal impediment.
- ❖ The minimum age for widow's benefits is 60, or 50 if disabled.

Widower
See Widow.

Work Credits
See Credits.

Worker
See Wage Earner.

INDEX

ABOUT THE AUTHOR

Kathleen Sindell, Ph.D. is the author of numerous academic, popular, and professional finance articles, Web sites, proposals, and books, including the bestselling reference book, "Investing Online for Dummies, Eds. 1-5" (listed for two consecutive years on the *Wall Street Journal's* Bestselling Business Book List). Sindell has an in-depth understanding of the financial services industry and holds Series 7, 63 and 65 licenses.

Dr. Sindell's public speaking and writings assist individuals in gaining financial literacy. Sindell tracks a variety of financial sources to identify emerging investor and personal finance trends then creates educational investor and finance presentations or materials for publishers, organizations, trade associations and educational institutions. Dr. Sindell is regularly tapped as a financial expert on ABC World News, The Nightly Business Report, and at popular online and print outlets.

Dr. Sindell has over 20 years of experience in designing and developing learning objectives, instructional activities and curriculum using adult learning principles and various media and tools to achieve maximum results in the shortest time. Kathleen Sindell, Ph.D. is certified to teach Business and Industrial Management, Banking and Finance by the California Board of Governors (Certificate #19507). For over four years she managed the Financial Management and Real Estate programs and faculty at the University of Maryland University College Graduate School. For 16 years Sindell was a practioner faculty member of the Johns Hopkins Carey School of Business, where she created graduate courses and taught the internet and e-commerce, corporate finance, individual investment management and personal wealth management.. Dr. Sindell is member of the Board of Directors for the Financial Planning Association, National Capital Area, a subcommittee member of the DC Council on Financial Literacy, and a member of the Greater Washington Jump$tart Coalition.

CPSIA information can be obtained at www.ICGtesting.com
Printed in the USA
BVOW03s2244030214

343884BV00008B/116/P